How to Do Everything with Your Scanner

2nd Edition

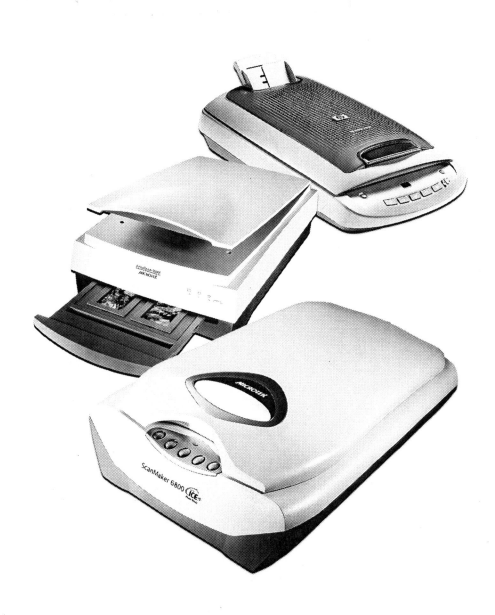

How to Do *Everything* with Your

Scanner

Second Edition

Dave Huss

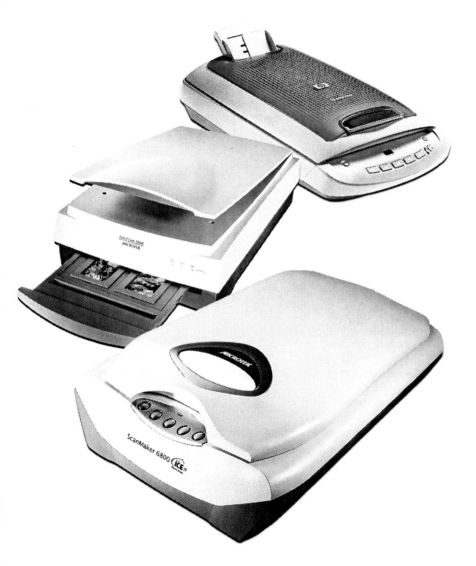

McGraw-Hill/Osborne

New York   Chicago   San Francisco
Lisbon   London   Madrid   Mexico City
Milan   New Delhi   San Juan
Seoul   Singapore   Sydney   Toronto

The McGraw·Hill Companies

McGraw-Hill/Osborne
2100 Powell Street, Floor 10
Emeryville, California 94608
U.S.A.

To arrange bulk purchase discounts for sales promotions, premiums, or fund-raisers, please contact **McGraw-Hill/Osborne** at the above address. For information on translations or book distributors outside the U.S.A., please see the International Contact Information page immediately following the index of this book.

How to Do Everything with Your Scanner
Second Edition

1234567890 FGR FGR 019876543

ISBN 0-07-222891-1

Publisher	Brandon A. Nordin
Vice President &	
Associate Publisher	Scott Rogers
Acquisitions Editor	Megg Morin
Senior Project Editor	LeeAnn Pickrell
Acquisitions Coordinator	Tana Allen
Technical Editor	Steve Bain
Copy Editor	Jan Jue
Proofreader	Mike McGee
Indexer	Karin Arrigoni
Computer Designers	Tara A. Davis, John Patrus
Illustrators	Melinda Moore Lytle, Michael Mueller, Lyssa Wald
Series Design	Mickey Galicia
Cover Series Design	Dodie Shoemaker

Cover image of Nikon CoolScan IV is courtesy Nikon Inc. Nikon and Coolpix are registered trademarks of Nikon Inc. © 2002 All rights reserved.
Cover image of HP 5500C is courtesy Hewlett-Packard Company.
Cover image of Epson Perfection 2450 is courtesy Epson America, Inc.

This book was composed with Corel VENTURA™ Publisher.

This book is dedicated to Jeff McDaniel—

Nearly a doctor…

Almost a son-in-law…

Already a great man.

About the Author

David Huss has been working with scanners for over a quarter-century. David has worked as a scanner consultant for many of the major scanner manufacturers and for several Fortune 100 companies. He has authored over 15 books on digital image editing that have been translated into eight languages. A popular conference speaker, he has taught scanning workshops in the U.S. and Europe and he has been seen on CNN and Tech TV. A third-generation Texan, he and his family have called Austin, Texas, their home for the past 30 years.

Contents at a Glance

Contents

Acknowledgments

This is my favorite part of the book because it is a secret area that very few readers ever delve into. I could put top national secrets in an acknowledgment page, and I am convinced they would be safer than if they were kept in a safe. Still, like the endless thank you speeches at the Academy Awards, these acknowledgments are an important and necessary part of the book-making process. So in the category of best performance in the role of an acquisitions editor…

The Envelope Please

The winner is Megg Morin. No big surprise here. She has been my acquisitions editor for more years than either of us will admit (publicly). She is a great editor and a good friend. In addition to being an editor, she now a brand new mom by giving birth to Cooper Morin just as the book was in its final stages. Now there are several winners in the category of best performance in a supporting role. They include a great graphics gal at Osborne, Lyssa Wald. It is her job to make the photos in this edition look good. Point in fact, I have been writing graphic books for over 12 years now, and she is one of the few graphics people who didn't think pixels were mystical winged creatures that fly in the enchanted forest at night. Major kudos to Lyssa. Others who helped with the book include Jan Jue who made it appear that I actually had a fundamental grasp of the English language, Mike McGee who proofread the book, Karin Arrigoni who created the index, Melinda Lytle who put together the color insert, and Kathleen Edwards and Kelly Stanton-Scott who, along with other folks in the Production department, took the raw manuscript and made it into the book you're reading now.

In a major supporting role is LeeAnn Pickrell. As project editor, her job is a little like the person beating the drum for the rowers inside the galley in the movie *Ben Hur.* She beats out a tempo that all the rest of us need to keep. Getting a book ready to ship to the printer is no small task because in addition to working with all of the staff involved in laying out the book and a hundred other things, she is working with authors who are out of her physical reach. As a group, authors are terrible people to get to deliver materials on time; the only exception I am aware is the technical editor, Steve Bain. I hate Steve because he is a very organized author who writes good books and delivers his manuscripts on time making the rest of us authors look bad. Even though I hate Steve, I have known him for more than eight years and consider him a good friend—but don't tell him that; it's our secret.

I must also include thanks to Amy Podurgiel at the MWW Group in New Jersey (let us pray) who is my main contact with Nikon and part of the reason the slide and negative scanning chapter is so complete. Speaking of film scanning, my thanks to all of the folk at Applied Science Fiction here in Austin for your input as well as the fine folk at Hewlett-Packard from which some of the finest scanners in the world are produced. Especially to Dr. Robert Gann who has forgotten more about scanners than I will learn in a lifetime.

I want to mention my regular co-workers at Motorola, most of whom had nothing at all to do with this book, but I really like them and thought they would like to see their name in print (and maybe they'll buy lots of copies of the book to give to friends): Mary Thomas (my boss), Kathy Flories, Shannon Osgood, Denise Fischer whose scrapbook I used throughout the book, Glenn Jones, and Nick Evans.

No author who has been married for more than a week forgets to thank his family for putting up with missed weekend trips, vacations, and seeing more of the back of his head than the front. To my lovely wife Elizabeth (approaching our 30th anniversary), my heartfelt thanks. To my daughter Grace (age 22), if this book sells really well you can have Diana Krall play at your wedding—really, really, really well. To my son Jon (age 27), thanks for letting me put all of the photos of you when you were a kid in the book; drinks are on me.

Cheers!
Dave Huss
Austin, Texas, 2003

Introduction

Scanners are powerful input devices that are now inexpensive enough to be used in both the home and the office. When I first began to work with scanners not so many years ago, they were so expensive that I provided clients with five-point checklist to see if their requirements could justify the cost of a scanner. Now you can buy a good scanner for $50.00 and a quality scanner for under $250. If you think your scanner is just for scanning flat things like photos, you are in for a pleasant shock. Inside the pages of this book are things to do with your scanner that you probably would have never thought possible. Did you know that your scanner could help you lose weight? Yes, it can. While holding the scanner in its box, climb fifty sets of stairs twice a day. OK, maybe it isn't the best weight reducer in the world, but when I think about what you can do with your scanner, I sometimes get carried away.

Who Should Read This Book?

Everyone who wants get the most out their scanner. This book is for everyone who wants to add a strong visual impact to his or her communications—both personal and professional. This book does not presume any special computer skills; in fact, if you have recently won the Nobel Prize for Computer Science, I don't think you will like the book—but since you want to spend the prize money on something, why not buy it as a gift for a friend?

What's in Each Part of the Book?

The book is divided into three parts to help you complete a course of self-study that will make you a scanner professional in no time.

- **Part I** introduces you to the world of scanners as it exists today. You will discover that there are many different kinds of scanners out there and how to select the best one to meet your scanning needs. You will also discover how to set up and maintain a scanner as the basics of achieving a good scan.

■ **Part II** is about putting your scanner to work in a variety of tasks and projects. These include scanning images for placement on the Web, converting printed text into electronic documents or faxes, and creating exciting family projects from scrapbooks to photo calendars.

■ **Part III** is for those who want to do even more with their scanner. In this part, you will discover how to scan slides and negatives to preserve them from loss or damage, and you will discover the power of photo editors and how they can be used to restore and preserve family heirlooms.

What Features and Benefits Are Included in This Book?

Many helpful editorial elements are presented in this book, including a checklist of how-to topics at the beginning of each chapter to let you know what's covered. Skip through these lists to find out what is relevant and interesting to you. The chapters of this book are fairly self-contained, and a detailed index is provided to help you review specific terms and concepts.

You'll also find step-by-step instructions, figures, and illustrations to guide you every step of the way. Other useful elements include

■ *Tips* that point out easier and more efficient ways to do projects and tasks

■ *Cautions* that warn of common errors and pitfalls

■ *Notes* that highlight additional relevant concepts

■ *How To* and *Did You Know* sidebars that contain useful additional information about the scanning process and equipment

The following conventions are used in this book:

■ *Click* means to click an item once using the left mouse button.

■ *Double-click* means to click an item twice in rapid succession using the left mouse button.

■ *Right-click* means to click an item once using the right mouse button.

Let Me Hear from You

As you read through this book and come up with ideas, drop me a line and let me know what you are doing with your scanner. Because of the volume of e-mail I receive from my other books, I cannot guarantee I will be able to answer technical questions or respond, but in most cases, I will get back to you. My e-mail address is dave@davehuss.com. You can also see the latest photos that I have posted by going to my web site at www.davehuss.com. The images at this site are updated every few weeks, depending on my schedule.

Part I

Basic Details about Your Scanner

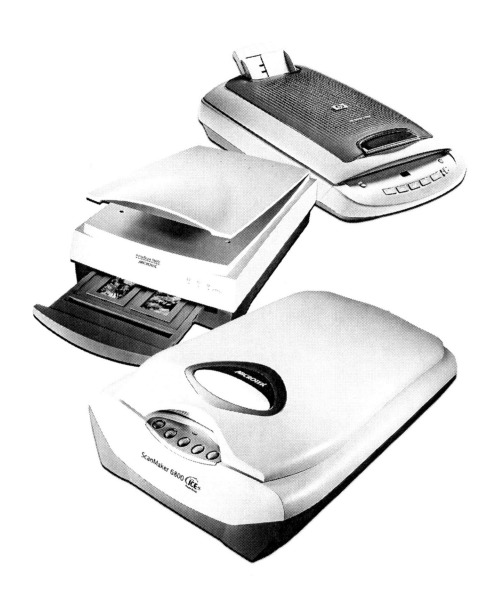

Chapter 1

Get Acquainted with Your Scanner

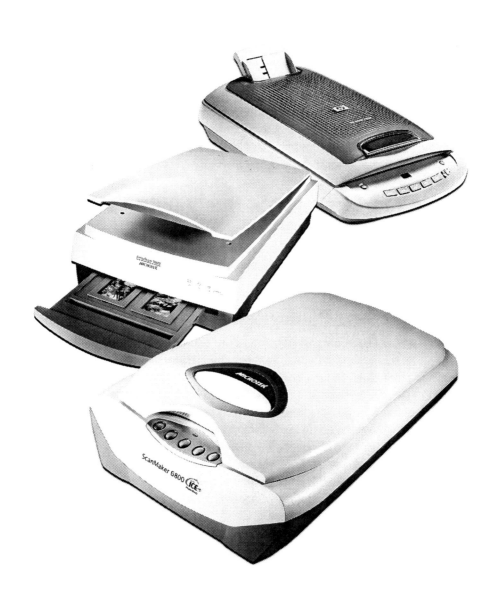

How to...

- Create both clever and mundane projects for your scanner
- Learn how scanning works
- Understand some scanner terms and concepts
- Survey the different kinds of scanners that are available

Not so long ago, scanners were really expensive, didn't do much, and what they did do, they didn't do very well. Installing a scanner interface card into a computer was a major undertaking, and what little software existed to control the scanner required enormous effort to accomplish even a simple scan of a photograph. But that was then and this is now. Today, a scanner that sells for less than $50 outperforms most scanners that sold for over $1,000 just a few years ago. Also, today's scanners are smarter and do most of the work for you, freeing you to be creative. With that said, let's see what you can do with these imaging marvels.

Learn What Your Scanner Is Designed to Do

In many cases the only limitation on what your scanner can do is your imagination. Most people think of a scanner as hardware for scanning pictures into their computers. While the primary use for a scanner is to scan photos, you can do many more things with your scanner.

Copy and Preserve Photographs

With digital cameras becoming so popular, many people have started making and sharing electronic photo albums. So what about that shoebox full of photos, negatives, and color slides in the closet? The scanner allows you to make them into computer files that can be printed or posted on the Web. You can also scan photos into your computer if for no other reason than to preserve them, such as the photo shown in Figure 1-1. Whether you are into the very popular hobby of scrapbooking or just want to preserve your photographic past, once a photo has been scanned, it can't fade, get scratched, bent, folded, or serve as the background for a budding young artist with a felt marker. Most importantly, awkward pictures of children are preserved for potential embarrassment or blackmail when they get older.

Capture Moments in Time

All of the wonderful works of art that adorn refrigerator doors, an example of which is shown in Figure 1-2, are prime candidates for a scanner. While creating a scrapbook is

FIGURE 1-1   Your scanner can preserve photographs and protect them from further aging.

a wonderful way to chronicle times and places in our lives, the materials in these books fade with time and are subject to the elements, fire, and flood. By scanning newspaper articles, great crayon impressions of the cat, concert tickets, or even the pages of your scrapbook with your scanner and burning them on a CD, you will have preserved them for posterity.

FIGURE 1-2   Preserving original art for future generations

Make the Pictures Better

Once a photograph has been scanned into the computer, any of dozens of programs on the market can make the photos look better or can restore them to their former glory. In some cases, improving the photo may entail something as simple as making an underexposed image lighter, like the one shown in Figure 1-3, or involve something a little more complex, like removing an old boyfriend from a great photo of you as shown in Figure 1-4.

Make Images Larger and Smaller

A scanner can also be used to make the photo, image, or any object being scanned either larger or smaller. This is an important feature of scanners that many users overlook. Enlarging or reducing an image on a scanner always produces superior results to doing the same thing with a software application.

Convert Printed Text into Electronic Text (OCR)

Just as a scanner can convert a photo into a graphics file, so your computer can convert printed text on paper into a word processing file. By using optical character recognition (OCR) software, your scanner can scan almost any printed document and convert it into text. What is more amazing, the OCR software available today allows you to scan a sheet of paper containing a long list of phone numbers like the one

FIGURE 1-3   Enhancing photos in a computer is pretty simple stuff.

FIGURE 1-4   Your computer can remove the former Mr. Right from a photo without using scissors.

shown in Figure 1-5 and convert it into an electronic document, saving hours of work and reducing the chance of errors.

Translate Printed Documents

Using OCR, your scanner can translate printed documents from one language to another. The software that does this is getting pretty sophisticated, and while I wouldn't recommend it for translating critical documents—like peace treaties with sovereign nations—they are wonderful for correspondence. Specialty hand-held scanners not much larger than a fat ballpoint pen can scan over a word and then show the translation in the liquid crystal display (LCD) on the scanner.

Add Business Cards to Address Books

Do you do a lot of work with business cards? I used to return from a major computer show with a stack of business cards over two inches thick. While there are scanners designed specifically to scan business cards, you can use your scanner with a dedicated software application to capture all of the information off of the business cards and put it into the address book of your personal digital assistant (PDA) or into one of your business applications like Outlook or one of the many contact applications like Act.

26 Support, warranty, and specifications

If the number below has changed, visit
http://www.hp.com/cposupport/mail_support.html to check for a new one.

Argentina 0810 555 5520 (5411) 4778 8380 (outside Argentina)	*Egypt* +202 7956222
	Finland +358 (0)203 47 288
Australia 03 8877 8000	*France* +33 (0)1 43 62 34 34
Austria 43 (0) 810 00 6080	*Germany* +49 (0)180 52 58 143 (24 PF/min)
Belgium Dutch: +32 (0)2 626 8806 French: +32 (0)2 626 8807	*Greece* +30 (0)1 619 64 11
Brazil (11) 3747 7799 (greater São Paulo) 0800 157 751 (outside greater São Paulo)	*Guatemala* 1 800 999 5305
	Hong Kong +85 (2) 3002 8555
Canada 905 206-4663	*Hungary* +36 (0)1 382 1111
Chile 800 22 5547 (Post-sales Business Computing) 800 360 999 (Post-sales Home Computing)	*India* +91 11 682 6035
	Indonesia +62 (21) 350 3408
China +86 (0) 10 6564 5959	*Ireland* +353 (0)1 662 5525
Colombia 9 800 919 477	*Israel* +972 (0)9 952 48 48
Czech Republic +42 (0)2 6130 7310	*Italy* +39 02 264 10350
Denmark +45 39 29 4099	*Japan* +81 3 3335 9800

FIGURE 1-5 This list of phone numbers can be scanned and, using OCR, converted to an electronic document.

Manage Your Documents Once They're Scanned

Not only can your scanner be used for OCR, but some applications also work with your scanner to convert printed documents to text files and to organize them. With such applications you can scan in your receipts, press releases, articles, or what have you, and they will be stored on your computer as electronic files. If this was all the programs did, they would be real timesavers. Another great feature of these applications is their ability to automatically make note of keywords such as dates, proper names, and so on, in the scanned documents. Later, when you are trying to find that article on the history of Elk Snoot, Montana, the application can locate it for you immediately and let you view it on your computer monitor or print it.

Copy Your Documents and Images

Most scanners sold today offer the ability to directly scan and print an image placed on the scanner glass. While this feature has always been available, it wasn't until the scanner manufacturers began adding dedicated buttons on the front of the scanners that this became as easy to operate as a copy machine.

Fax Your Documents

With the increasing popularity of e-mail, the fax machine is used less and less. Still, when you need to fax a document, it's nice to know that most scanners can be used as a high-quality fax machine. This capability allows you to send and receive faxes without having to purchase a fax machine. All you need besides your scanner and computer is a phone line and a fax modem card in your computer. Most computers manufactured since 1998 include fax-capable modems. Like the copy feature described earlier, just about every scanner sold today offers this fax feature.

Scan 3-D Objects

Because most of us have a flatbed scanner, it is easy to fall into the trap of thinking that everything that the scanner scans must be flat. Actually, nothing could be further from the truth. Your flatbed scanner is essentially a digital camera without a zoom lens. Almost anything you can place on a scanner can be successfully scanned and made into a graphic file. This provides a quick way to capture an image for something that you wish to sell through an online auction like eBay. Some of the more obvious things to scan include coin and stamp collections, because they are essentially flat. Do you have hand-painted plates made by a loved one or some hand-crafted items like lace, counted cross-stitch, or embroidery? All these items can be placed on a scanner and their images preserved even if they don't fit under the lid. (The lid on most scanners lifts off.)

You can also scan 3-D objects such as the antique Chinese teapot shown in Figure 1-6. In addition, you can make great floral arrangements on the scanner by putting the flowers on the scanner and placing a complementary-colored paper or cloth over them to produce a lovely image for a greeting card or newsletter. The weight and height of the object on the scanner limit how large an object you can scan. For example, a person sitting on the scanner would probably break it, or an object that is a foot tall would have its sides out of focus.

Besides all of the functions that have already been mentioned, you can do many more things with your scanner. These capabilities will be discussed throughout the book. Now let's take a peek under the hood (so to speak) and discover how a scanner does what it does.

FIGURE 1-6   You can even scan 3-D objects like this antique Chinese teapot.

The Hows and Whys of Scanning

Scanners are simple devices, as you can see from Figure 1-7, and they operate much like an office copier.

1. You place an image face down on the scanner glass. Beneath the glass is a light source that is connected to a scanning mechanism; together they are called a *scan head.*

2. The scanner uses a small motor to move the scan head under the image that is placed on the copy glass. The scan head's sensor captures the light that reflects off the image. The head can read very small portions of the image—less than $1/120,000^{th}$ of a square inch.

3. A *CCD sensor* in the scan head acts as the recording device. ("CCD" stands for "charge coupled device," which is the type of sensor used in scanners and digital cameras.) The sensor captures the reflected light and converts it into electrical signals. These signals are converted into computer bits (called *pixels*) and sent to your computer.

That's all there is to scanning—really. Still, it's beneficial to know some of the jargon used by scanner manufacturers and users. You'll learn about these terms in the next section.

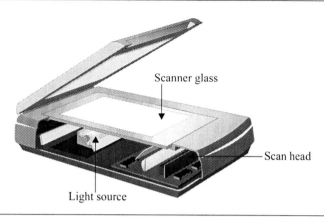

Scanner glass

Scan head

Light source

FIGURE 1-7   The inside of a scanner contains very few parts.

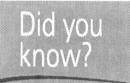

Your Scanner Only Sees in Black and White

Your color scanner can't see color. It's true. The CCD sensor can only measure the amount of light striking it regardless of the color. To make these grayscale sensors produce color requires that the reflected light from the image be broken down into the three primary computer colors: red, green, and blue (RGB). To do this, most scanners have three identical rows of sensors in the scan head. Each row is covered with a different colored filter of red, green, or blue. All three sets of information (called *channels*) are then converted to bits and sent to the computer, which passes the information to each of the RGB channels of your monitor. The result appears as a color image. More expensive scanners focus the reflected light through a prism, which breaks the light down to its component parts, and each color strikes its respective row of CCD sensors. The advantage of this more expensive approach is that the color rendition is better. Unlike the colored filters, which tend to become more opaque with age, the prism maintains crisp color definition—assuming someone doesn't drop the scanner and misalign the scan head.

Scanner Terms and Concepts You Should Understand

Whether you are talking about car engines or makeup, every field has its own terminology. Scanners have their own buzzwords as well, and it would be useful to understand them and how they apply to buying or using a scanner.

Pixels

The smallest piece of a digital picture, *pixels* are often referred to as the building blocks of digital images. Much as a mosaic tile image (like the one shown in Figure 1-8) is composed of hundreds, if not thousands, of colored tiles, so a digital image is composed of thousands, if not millions, of uniformly square pixels arranged in a checkerboard pattern. If you own or have looked at ads for digital cameras, you have already been exposed to the term. The first thing we discuss when talking about digital cameras is how many millions of pixels (megapixels) the camera can capture.

You need to know two facts about pixels. One, they are square and can only display one color at a time. The other thing to understand about pixels is that they do not come in a fixed size like other units of measure such as inches or centimeters.

FIGURE 1-8   Like this mosaic tile picture, digital images are made up of tiny parts called pixels.

For example, one pixel on one of the giant stadium TVs can be several feet wide, while a pixel from a scanned color slide can have a width of 1/8000th of an inch. The size of a pixel is controlled by our next topic—resolution.

Resolution

Easily the most misused term in computer graphics, *resolution* defines the density of pixels. Said another way, resolution tells how many pixels must fit into an inch or other unit of measure. Here is an example: Assume we have an image 1,000 pixels wide. If the resolution of the display device is set to 1,000 pixels per inch (ppi), the image will appear 1 inch wide. If the resolution is decreased to 100 ppi, the same image will appear to be 10 inches wide. Even though the display made the pixels in the image appear ten times larger, the image still contains 1,000 pixels. From this we can see a relationship between image size and resolution:

- ■ If the resolution is increased, the displayed or printed size of the image decreases.

- ■ If the resolution is decreased, the displayed or printed output size of the image increases.

We will discover more about resolution in the next chapter, but for now you only need to understand the relationship between resolution and output size.

Color Depth

The second-most-advertised technical feature of a scanner is the *color depth*. Most scanners capture three primary colors: red, green, and blue (RGB). The number of different shades of each color the scanner can capture determines how many colors the scanner can scan. For example, the output of most scanners has historically been 24-bit color. What this means is that the color for each of the three colors (channels) is limited to the number of different shades that can be expressed by 24 bits, which is roughly 16.7 million colors. Most scanners offer color depths that are greater than 24-bit color. While it seems reasonable that a greater color depth would produce superior color, the quality difference between a scan produced with a 24-bit and a 48-bit scanner can rarely be seen with the naked eye.

The principal advantage of increased color depth is its ability to capture a greater range of colors, but more importantly, some scanners can pass this 48-bit information to applications that can work with the greater color depth and extract greater image detail from the scan. This type of work is usually done by professionals who have large computers and lots of time and experience.

Color Space

Also called "color mode" or "color model," *color space* determines the way your scanner and computer see the colors in your scan. All scanners allow you to select the color space as shown in Figure 1-9. To make the scanning experience user-friendly, most scanning software interfaces enable you to select the type of image you are scanning, and from that choice the correct color mode is selected. For example, if you select printed text, the scanner software will internally set up the scanner for line art. Be aware that these preset color space settings are general selections and may not always be the best ones for the image you are scanning. In Chapter 3, you will learn more about selecting the correct color mode.

While there are over a dozen color modes, the following are the most common.

Line Art

This is also called "black and white." (Adobe calls it a "one color bitmap.") You may also see it referred to as "1-bit color." Whatever the name, it describes an image that only has two colors. A classic example of this is a standard business card or a sheet of text printed with a laser printer. Be aware that when the term "black-and-white" is used to describe a movie or television show way back when, it is actually referring to grayscale, which is the next color mode discussed.

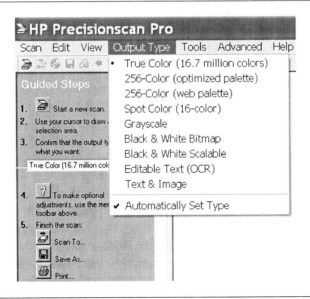

FIGURE 1-9   Most scanning software offers many choices for color space.

Grayscale

Like line art, grayscale mode has only one color (black), but it has 256 different shades. A black-and-white photograph scanned into a computer image is an example of a grayscale image.

256 Color

This color space also has several names. A favorite color space on the Internet, it is also called "8-bit color" or "indexed color." An image in 8-bit color is composed of up to 256 different colors. Depending on the number of colors in the original image, displaying an image with a palette of 256 colors can at times make a color photograph look like the Sunday comics and at other times look just like the original. This topic is covered in greater detail in Chapter 6.

 *Even if an image is to be used on the Web, you should never scan it at 256 colors if you plan to do any editing on it after you scan it.*

RGB Color

RGB color space wins the prize for most names. It is also called "24-bit color," "16.7 million," "millions of colors" (by HP), "true color," and many more. This is the color mode of choice for all color scanning. This gives your scanned color image a large enough palette of colors that the scanner can faithfully represent all the colors of the original.

Different Kinds of Scanners

Nearly every scanner that you encounter will be a flatbed scanner. Still, it is useful to be aware of the other scanners that are out there if only so you won't be confused the next time you talk to your printer, service bureau, or Kinko's.

Desktop Scanners

Most desktop scanners are flatbeds. They come in all shapes and sizes, a few of which are shown in Figure 1-10. What they all have in common is their general overall shape. A flatbed has a flat copy glass under which a light source moves below the object being scanned. Some flatbeds have dedicated options like an automatic document feeder (ADF) providing automated scanning of multiple documents. Other flatbeds offer either built-in or external attachments for scanning film negatives or color slides and which have a misleading name. They are called

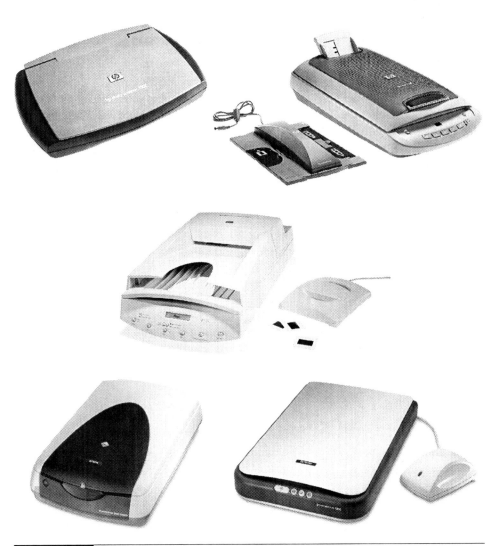

FIGURE 1-10   Flatbed scanners come in all shapes and sizes.

"transparency adapters," which has made more than one user think they were for scanning overhead transparencies. Some flatbed scanners are small or thin or both. Others are oversized so that they can scan large images like maps and large architectural CAD drawings. Still others are designed for use by printing professionals and cost several thousand dollars. The most expensive type of scanner isn't a flatbed at all; it's a scanner called a drum scanner.

 *Any equipment or software that is designed for use in the production of material that is to be printed on an offset press is referred to as "prepress."*

Drum Scanners

When J.P. Morgan was asked how much his new yacht cost, he replied, "If you have to ask the price, you can't afford it." The same can be said of the drum scanner. They are large, cost more than your car, and may require more than one operator. Still, while you probably will never come into contact with these scanning behemoths, you will hear about them all the time. See Figure 1-11 and the sidebar "Did You Know What a Drum Scanner Is?" to learn a little bit about them and what makes them so famous.

Film Scanners

While still more expensive than flatbed scanners, film scanners are dedicated scanners, such as the ones shown in Figure 1-12, that are designed specifically to scan film negatives and colors slides. In the last few years, the number of manufacturers making film scanners has increased tenfold, and the price of these devices has dropped dramatically. If you have lots of color slides or film negatives sitting around in a shoebox, an investment in a film scanner may be a wise decision. Another candidate for a good film scanner is the photographer who is still shooting film but wants to manipulate photos in Photoshop rather than in a darkroom.

Photo courtesy of Heidelberg.

FIGURE 1-11   The Heidelberg Primescan D drum scanner is used to create high-quality scans for prepress.

FIGURE 1-12   These film scanners are designed to convert film negatives and color slides into computer images.

If you have made the switch from film to digital camera and have a large collection of film negatives and slides, consider buying a film scanner, scanning all of your existing film negatives/slides, and then reselling the scanner at an online auction like eBay.

The Drum Scanner

A drum scanner isn't actually used to scan drums. This costly scanner consists of a rapidly spinning glass cylinder to which an image is taped on the inside. A light source is beamed through the image on the drum and is read by a photo-multiplier tube (PMT). Invented back in 1949, a PMT is a vacuum tube containing a phosphor sensor. The PMT produces a high signal-to-noise ratio (S/N), which is a technical way of saying it produces the highest quality scan.

As good as images from a drum scanner are, a few difficulties are associated with them (other than their price tag). It is necessary to mount the slide or negative with a thin film of mineral oil or naphthalene. Of course, after the scan is completed, the coating must be removed.

Specialty Scanners

These are scanners that are designed for specific functions. While they are not often seen in retail sales outlets, they are nonetheless great productivity tools for the jobs that they do.

Hand-Held Scanners

This category of scanner includes units that are the size of a fat felt marker and can scan one word or one line of text at a time (see Figure 1-13). What they do with the scanned text depends on what this hand scanner was designed to do. Some will scan in the text, perform OCR (convert it to text that can be pasted into a word processing document), and then transfer it into a computer. Others are handy dictionaries; they have a small LCD display on the side of the pen and will translate the scanned word into another language. This is a great help when you are reading a document in another language and you cannot remember the definition of a word. You can scan the word and see the definition rather than thumbing through a dictionary. This type of scanner also includes bar code scanners, which are no longer tools used only by large corporations. Many small office/home office (SOHO) applications support the generation and reading of bar codes.

Business Card Scanners

These dedicated scanners do one thing and they do it very well. Stick a business card in the scanner, and this jewel will read the card, extract all of the information on the card, and put it into your address book on the computer or your PDA. The model shown in Figure 1-14 can scan the logos off of the cards, and others even scan in color.

FIGURE 1-13   Hand-held scanners perform a variety of specialized functions.

FIGURE 1-14   This dedicated scanner can extract business card data into your computer or PDA.

Now that you have learned a little about scanners and what they can do, in the next chapter you will discover everything you need to know to buy, install, and maintain your scanner.

Chapter 2

Buy, Install, and Maintain Your Scanner

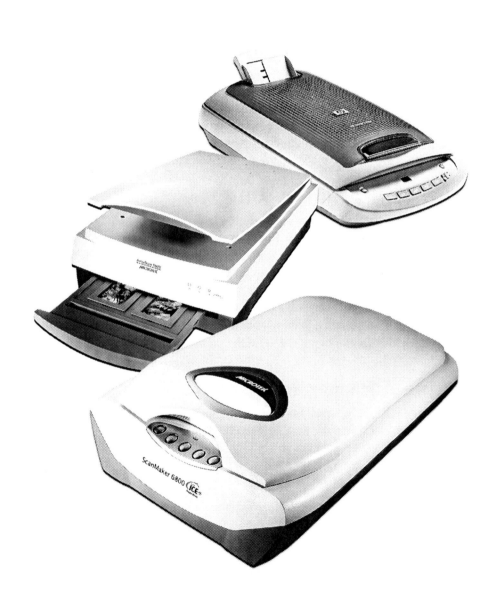

How to...

■ Decide which scanner best fits your needs

■ Read scanner technical information

■ Install your scanner software

■ Install the scanner hardware and test it

Now that you know something about how a scanner works and a smattering of relevant terminology, you can use that knowledge to get the best scanner to suit your needs. This chapter will examine the tasks that you want to accomplish with a scanner and find out what type of scanner provides the best price/performance match. We will also look at what other equipment is required in the way of a computer and take a peek at some doodads that may surprise you.

What Scanner Is Best for You?

Many different models of scanners are available in the marketplace. Often you'll find several different scanner models from the same manufacturer, and they'll all look alike. Only when you look at the technical gibberish on the side of the box will you see the differences between those seemingly identical units. Once you know what the differences are, you must decide if the extra features are worth the extra money. Yes, it can be a daunting task to determine which scanner best meets your needs, but in the following sections we will go through a decision process that hopefully will help you to get the most for your scanner buck.

What Type of Scanner Do You Need?

The first question to ask yourself is: What is it that I will mostly be doing with the scanner? Some things a scanner may be used to scan include

■ Photographs

■ Film negatives or color slides

■ Printed matter (OCR)

■ 3-D Objects

■ Family heirlooms and memorabilia

Most people will use the scanner for scanning photos and maybe some other items. If, on the other hand, you primarily want to scan film negatives and slides, then you should definitely consider buying a dedicated film scanner, which will produce the best quality scans of this media. The disadvantage of these scanners is that they can only scan slides and negatives. If you want to scan photos and some slides and negatives, then consider getting one of the photo scanners that include a transparency unit (TPU); this way you can scan in photos as well as film and negatives.

Some high-end photo scanners are designed specifically for professional photographers who have yet to make the transition to digital cameras but still require digital images. These are flatbed scanners that can scan multiple sizes of negatives at resolutions up to 10,000 dpi.

What Size Scanner Do You Need?

What size scanner you need refers to the maximum size of document that can be scanned. Most scanners have a scanning area that is A4 or U.S. letter size (8.5×11 inches). This size of scanning area (also called the "reading area") meets most needs, unless you need to scan in documents that are legal size (8.5×14 inches). In addition, some specialty scanners have a scanning area large enough to scan an entire tabloid page (11×17 inches), and wide format scanners are capable of scanning large CAD drawings, maps, and architectural drawings up to E size (36×48 inches). While working on this book, I discovered that libraries use wide format scanners to scan newspapers for archival purposes. These scanners are wide enough to scan an entire unfolded page at once. These are called *wide format scanners* and are not flatbed scanners at all; they look like the one shown in Figure 2-1.

Should You Buy a New, Refurbished, or Used Scanner?

I love getting a bargain as much as anyone, but when it comes to scanners, the prices have dropped and the performance increased so much over the past few years that any used scanner will probably not be a good choice. For example, I have a scanner in my garage that was a high-end prepress scanner in 1993 and sold for over $2,000. I saw several on eBay last week, and the sellers were not able to get more than $20 for them.

Refurbished scanners can be a great bargain, and most scanner manufacturers have an area on their web site where they can be purchased. An important piece of advice when buying a refurbished or closeout scanner is to compare the price and specifications of the scanner being offered with similar new scanners. Because the prices of scanners continue to drop, sometimes the discounted price is still more than the equivalent new scanner. The other consideration when looking at a refurbished— also called previously owned, remanufactured, and (my favorite) previously loved— scanner is the warranty offered. Some companies offer the original warranty, while 90-day warranties are also common.

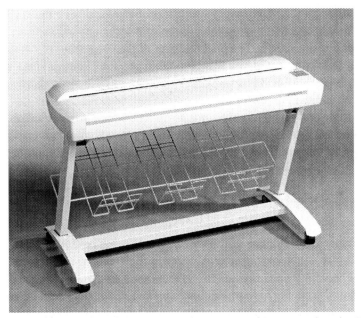

Photo courtesy of Contex.com Scanning Technology.

FIGURE 2-1   A wide format scanner can scan in documents up to 50 inches across.

Where Should You Buy Your Scanner?

There is no pat answer to this question. The advantage of buying on the Internet is that often it is cheaper, and in most cases you save the local sales tax. But remember that the shipping charges could cost you more than your sales tax savings. Your local computer store or office superstore has employees to answer your questions, but the odds of them knowing anything about scanners (other than the price) are pretty remote. This doesn't make them evil or stupid; it is just that so little profit margin is left in selling scanners that the stores cannot afford to have experts on the floor to answer your questions. This same store also has many scanners displayed, but they are not hooked up to anything, so you don't have the opportunity to do test scans. But ask yourself what you would look for, anyway. Scanners have become commodity items—meaning that a scanner from Epson will perform much the same as the equivalent scanner from HP, although both companies would dispute my conclusion.

Which Scanner Interface Is Best?

The interface your scanner uses to connect to your computer affects how fast your scanner can capture an image. Only a few years ago, the parallel port interface was

CHAPTER 2:   Buy, Install, and Maintain Your Scanner   **25**

2

the most common interface for consumer scanners, while the SCSI (Small Computer Standard Interface) port was the only choice of high-end scanners. Today the most popular scanner interface is USB 1.1 (Universal Serial Bus). While SCSI is still used, IEEE 1394 (FireWire) and USB 2.0 are being used on more and more high-end scanners.

The scanner interface you need is determined by what interfaces are available on your computer. If you are still using Windows 95, you cannot use USB or IEEE 1394. Your only choices are parallel port and SCSI. (You will need to install a SCSI card.) Windows 98, Me, XP, and Windows 2000 operating systems support USB and IEEE 1394, but again, your computer must have the hardware (either built-in or as an add-on card). The speed of the data transfers is measured in the number of 8-bit words (bytes) that can be moved in a second. The speed difference between the different interfaces is shown in Table 2-1.

If your computer doesn't have a USB interface, an add-on card is pretty inexpensive—less than $25 for a USB 1.1 PCI card. Don't forget that your computer must have Windows 98 or later installed to use a USB card. While Windows 2000 supports USB and IEEE 1394, Windows NT doesn't. If you can't decide between adding an IEEE 1394 adapter or USB, consider that although the IEEE 1394 adapters are only a little more expensive than USB adapters, the number of peripherals that use the IEEE 1394 interface is much smaller than those that use USB. There are also USB and IEEE 1394 PCMCIA cards for adding this feature to notebooks.

How Much Resolution Do You Need?

Resolution used to be a big selling point for scanners a few years back. Now almost every scanner offers astronomical resolution figures. How much resolution do you need? For scanning photos and other images, you need a lot less than you might imagine. Most images are scanned at 200 to 300 dots per inch (dpi). Surprised? If

Interface	Maximum Transfer Speed (Megabytes per Second)	Speed Factor (Compared to Parallel)
Parallel	0.1 MBps	—
ECP/EPP Parallel	3 MBps	26 times faster
USB 1.0/1.1	1.5 MBps	13 times faster
USB 2.0	60 MBps	522 times faster
SCSI-2	20 MBps	174 times faster
IEEE 1394	50 MBps	435 times faster

TABLE 2-1   Interface Choices—SCSI, USB 1/2, Parallel, FireWire/1394/iLink

Different USBs Are Compatible

Technically, three USB specifications are available (USB 1.0, 1.1, and 2.0).
The first USB interface was originally known just as USB. After a year, many
improvements were made to it and it became 1.1. To save confusion, both the 1.0
and 1.1 are lumped together into 1.1. The newer USB 2.0 can communicate with
a computer equipped with USB 1.1, but the interface will operate at the slower
USB data rate. So if your scanner has a USB 2.0 interface and your computer
only has the older USB connection, it will work. Though USB 2.0 uses the same
cables and connectors as USB 1.1, you may run into cables that cause problems
connecting high-speed peripherals. To avoid potential problems, most vendors
include USB 2.0–compliant cables with their USB 2 peripherals; if they don't,
you should buy one.

your scanner offers the ability to scan film negatives or slides, then the higher
resolutions of 2400–4800 dpi are necessary. This is because you need a higher
resolution to scan something as small as a 35mm negative into something as large
as an 8×10 photo. Still, there are a few things about resolution to be aware of when
reading scanner specifications.

FireWire, IEEE 1394, and iLink Are the Same

First there was FireWire, which was invented by Apple. Over 400 times
faster than USB 1.1, FireWire became the interface of choice for digital video
camcorders. Soon companies began using it for other external devices that
benefited from the high-speed throughput of the interface, like scanners and
external drives. So why weren't they called FireWire? Because Apple owns the
name and is very restrictive in allowing non-Apple vendors to use it. Soon it
became a standard (IEEE 1394), which has come to be known as 1394. That
leaves iLink, which is the Sony brand name for the same interface.

The Resolution Number Game

When reading the resolution on the scanner specifications, you may discover that the resolution is expressed in an odd format. What would you think of resolution data that says, "1200×2400 dpi"? It is telling you that the scanner's recording head has a resolution of 1200 dpi. So, where did the "2400 dpi" come from? In the first chapter, you learned that the scanning head is moved under the scanner glass during the scan. Mounted on a rubber belt, the scanning head is run by a special motor that can move it in very tiny steps. The result is that the resolution in one direction is twice the resolution of the other. How can you make use of this extra resolution? You can't. So, when you have two numbers that describe the resolution of a scanner, the lower number of the two will be the real resolution, and the only value that should interest you.

The other fuzzy area of the resolution game has to do with the fact that there are two ways to describe the resolution of a scanner. The true resolution of the scanner is called the *optical resolution*. The scanner can also "read between the lines," so to speak, and effectively double or triple the apparent resolution through a process called *interpolation*. The scanner specifications used to list this resolution information as an interpolated figure, but now it is listed in a more subtle fashion, calling it *input resolution* (optical) and *output resolution* (interpolated).

How Deep Does Your Color Need to Be?

Scanners list how many colors they can capture by describing their color depth using the number of bits used to express each color. The more bits, the greater number of colors can be captured. There are several technical advantages to the increased color depth, but explaining how it works is a lengthy technical topic that would bore you and give me a headache. The important question to ask is: How many bits of color depth do you need? Any scanner on the market today has more color depth than is necessary for most applications.

One aspect of color depth and scanners should be briefly discussed. Most of the scanners that offer 30-, 36-, and 40-bit color depth can only capture that depth of color, but they then process it and send 24-bit color to the computer. Nothing is wrong with this since only a few photo-editing programs can work with images that have a greater color depth. Some scanners (and digital cameras) offer the ability to send the data from the recording head to the computer. Typically, this is called *raw data,* and people who do commercial photo retouching and other prepress people need the extra information in the image when they manipulate the image (through color correction, tonal adjustments, and so on). Although the raw data can be sent to the computer and used by the photo editing program, at some point it must be converted to 24-bit RGB data.

What Other Factors Should You Consider?

After you have gone through the items mentioned in the previous sections and have narrowed your search to a few choices, here are a few other things to keep in mind before you make your purchase.

Is the Scanner Manufacturer Reputable?

Buying from a well-known company is important for two reasons. First, if the scanner breaks, you have someone who will actually answer their phones and get you a replacement scanner. Second, a well-established company continues to update the scanner drivers when new operating systems are introduced. Buying a scanner from a company you have never heard of, like Lucky Happy Moon Scanners, Ltd., can be a real crapshoot and is not recommended.

What Software Is Included with the Scanner?

All vendors offer an assortment of software to add more apparent value to their scanner. In many cases, the software that has been included is a limited-feature version (usually indicated by "LE" for "limited edition" somewhere in its title), an older version of the application, or a timed full-featured evaluation version that will stop working promptly after 30 days unless you pay for the application.

Scanner Installation

Installing a scanner on a computer used to be nightmarish. It involved adding a scanner interface card to the computer and all of the other adjustments necessary to make the new card work. Today, if you follow the directions that came with your scanner, installing one is a pretty simple affair that is divided into two parts—software and hardware. You must first install the software, so that when you plug the scanner into the computer, the operating system will have all it needs to complete the installation of the scanner.

Here is a summary of the steps needed to install your scanner:

1. Place the scanner where it is to be located.

2. Unlock the transit lock. (They all have them.)

3. Connect the power but not the USB or IEEE 1394 cable to the computer.

4. Install the scanner software.

5. Connect the USB/1394 cable to the computer when requested by the installation software or after the software installation is complete.

6. Perform a test scan to make sure everything works.

7. Update the scanning software from the manufacturer's support site.

8. After completing the update, perform a final test scan.

Finding the Best Location for Your Scanner

You should give some thought to where to put your scanner before parking it somewhere in your office. First, the surface should be flat. Next, if you're going to scan images only occasionally, then the scanner location isn't critical. On the other hand, if you plan on doing lots of scanning, you should consider a location that places the scanner within easy reach of the computer. If the best location is too far for the interface cable to reach the computer, buy a longer cable. The extra money you spend for the cable will save you lots of money on medical bills that would be the natural result of playing the scanner version of Twister from your chair.

 *Never lay objects, especially heavy objects like books, on top of your scanner. If you do, it can actually misalign or damage the scanner.*

Unlocking and Connecting the Scanner

Every scanner has a *transit lock* that prevents the scan head from sliding around inside the scanner while it is being moved. The scan head must be unlocked before the scanner is powered up, or the scanner will make terrible noise as the locked scan head tries to move and may possibly damage the scanner. Over the past few years, designers have created some innovative designs that make it impossible to plug the power cord into the scanner until the scanner is unlocked. Plug the interface cable into the scanner, but do not plug it into the computer.

There are several new small scanners that do not need to be plugged into an AC outlet; instead, they draw their power from the USB bus. These scanners are referred to as USB-powered, and they cannot be plugged into a USB hub unless the hub is self-powered. You can identify a self-powered hub by the power adapter connected to it.

Installing Scanner Software

This is pretty much an automatic operation. The only options that you will face during installation are the choices as to whether you want to install the optional software that was included with your scanner. A good rule to follow when deciding about the free software is to ask yourself if you need it or will use it. This is your decision, of course, but I recommend that you only install the software necessary to use the scanner. You can always install the other software later.

Why You Shouldn't Connect the Scanner Too Soon

If you plug a scanner or any other peripheral into a scanner running Windows 98 or later, the operating system will automatically detect the device, and if the scanner software has not been installed, the operating system will load a Windows Image Acquisition (WIA) driver for the scanner. The idea of the WIA sounds good, but it actually is a primitive interface that doesn't allow access to many scanner features.

Attaching the Scanner and Making a Scan

At some point during the software installation, you will be asked to plug in the scanner or to turn it on. When the computer detects the scanner, it will complete the scanner installation. Then, make a test scan to verify it works correctly. Even if you just bought your scanner, there could be updates available from the manufacturer. If there are updates, download them, install them, and after the update is complete, restart the computer and do another preview scan.

After you have done this, you are ready and able to begin scanning stuff. Which works out great, since that is the topic of the next chapter.

Chapter 3

Make Your First Scan

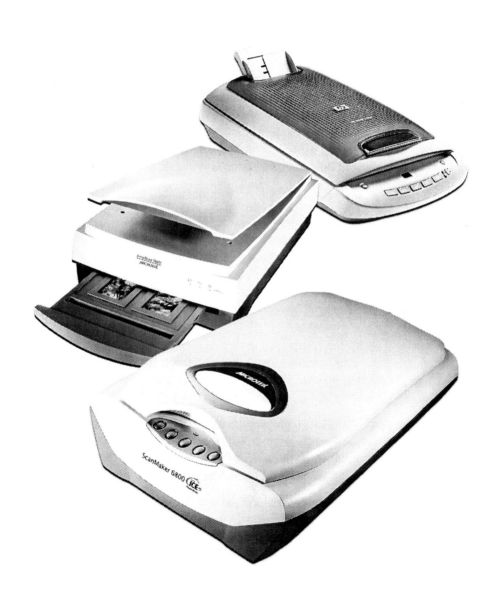

How to...

- Prepare an image to be scanned
- Discover different ways to begin scanning
- Get better scans with auto features turned off
- Evaluate the scan
- Work with copyrighted material

Scanners today are fantastic. They can scan at higher resolutions and capture a greater range of colors than scanners that were made only a few years ago. But regardless of how good they get, many scanned images don't look as good as they should, simply because the image or the scanner wasn't properly prepared before it was scanned. In this chapter, we will discuss the simple steps needed to prepare an image to be scanned and how to evaluate the completed scan.

Tools You Need Near Your Scanner

The tools needed to prepare the scanner and the images you are scanning are common household items, and the actual procedures are simple. The problem is, when it is time to scan something, very few people, if any, will take these necessary steps unless the tools are conveniently located near the scanner. I keep all of mine (see Figure 3-1) in a small plastic basket next to my scanner. The necessary tools are as follows:

- **Glass cleaner**   I recommend keeping it in a small spray bottle. Any brand will do, unless you saw the movie *My Big Fat Greek Wedding*—then you understand that Windex is the only logical choice.

- **Lint-free cloth**   There are many expensive paper and cloth products labeled lint-free, and while paper towels work as well as most, I get the best results using old undershirts. They have been through the dryer so many times that they are soft and functionally lint-free.

- **Soft brush**   Most photo stores have several excellent brushes designed specifically for photos. Some are antistatic; others are very wide, to make brushing the entire photo an easier task. While these are good, I have found that the brush that comes with blush makeup works just as well, with the understanding that it is a stiff brush and must be applied lightly—and never use one that has been used to apply blush.

- **Plastic triangle**   This is used for aligning photos. I use two different sizes, but just about any small one will do.

- **Pad of graph paper**   Used for aligning photos on scanner glass. Get a cheap pad of graph paper and not the expensive paper made for drafters.

- **Restickable adhesive glue stick**   This is the same adhesive used for those little Post-it notes that are stuck all over our lives. It is used when aligning photos.

Now that you are properly armed, let's see how to prepare an image for scanning.

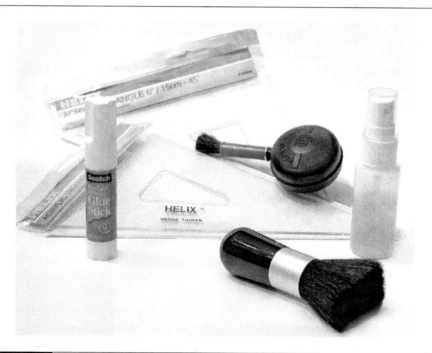

FIGURE 3-1   Here are some of the scanning tools that will improve the quality of your scans.

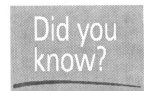

Why Canned Air Isn't Always the Best Choice

One popular way to remove dust and debris from a photo or scanner is to give it a blast with canned air (also called "compressed air"). While nothing is inherently wrong with using these pneumatic blasters, you should be aware of some drawbacks. First, blowing air across a photo can produce a static charge on the photo, which tends to attract more dust. Giving the scanner a blast to remove debris scatters it on anything near the scanner. Third, canned air is a far more expensive solution than the traditional ones discussed in this chapter. I keep a can of air handy to blow out my keyboard on occasion and for precious little else.

Three Steps of Scanning Preparation

As you read through this section, it may appear that it takes a long time to prepare an image for scanning, and I do not want to make scanning laborious. My experience has been that once you know what to do, it takes less than a minute to prepare for the first scan and less than 15 seconds to prep subsequent scans. Making the scanner and the image ready to be scanned involves the following three steps:

1. Clean the scanner glass, if necessary.

2. Remove dust and debris from the photo.

3. Align the photo on the scanner glass.

How to Clean the Scanner Glass

The scanner glass only need be cleaned at the beginning of a scanning session, unless you are scanning in 3-D objects like fudge brownies or soup. Just kidding about the soup—don't scan soup.

Use a glass cleaner applied to a soft cloth—do not spray it or pour it directly on the scanner glass. Every scanner manufacturer has their preferences for glass cleaners. For example, Hewlett-Packard (HP) recommends glass cleaners that don't contain ammonia, and Microtek recommends using alcohol. The important point is to clean the glass and not leave any streaks on it. The best way to check is to lift the lid of the scanner when the scanning light is on and look for streaking.

 *If your scanner recommends alcohol for scanner glass cleaning, use isopropyl rather than rubbing alcohol. The latter contains oils like lanolin and will leave a film on your scanner glass.*

Do not scratch the scanner glass. Be aware that most cheap paper towels have a coarse texture that can create fine scratches on the scanner glass. If you cannot find an old T-shirt or its equivalent, high-quality paper towels will do the trick.

Dealing with Foggy Scanner Glass

When inspecting the scanner glass, you might make a surprising discovery—the glass may appear to be fogged on the underside of the glass. Don't panic, it is normal and in almost all cases does not have an adverse affect on the resulting scan. Unless your scanner manufacturer provides specific directions on how to remove and clean the underside of the scanner glass, leave it alone.

Cleaning the Image

For photos, the most important step is to brush off any dust or debris with a soft brush. This is especially critical before scanning negatives or color slides, because the greater enlargement factor used for these small images can cause specks of dust to appear to be the size of cotton balls on the resulting scan. A variety of materials and techniques can be used to effectively lessen the dirt and grime from the photograph's surface.

TIP *Always handle photos and negatives by their edges. If you are going to be doing a lot of scanning with either photos or negatives, I recommend buying a pair of white cotton gloves at your local photo store. They are inexpensive and they make handling photos and negatives simpler.*

Dust and debris can be stubborn stuff, and you may discover that its eviction from the photo, slide, or negative can be a little challenging. Gently brush the dust off the photo, taking care not to scratch the photo surface. In Figure 3-1, you will notice that one of my brushes has a little squeeze bulb on it to blow the dust away while brushing it. If the dust is clinging to the photo, the humidity in the room is probably pretty low. The photo may have a static charge on it, turning your photo into a dust magnet. Be patient, the dust will come off. If you are experiencing physical problems with the image such as a curled panorama or a photo that is damaged, you will find several techniques for photographic rescue and restoration in Chapter 15.

Cleanliness Is a Real Timesaver

All of this attention to cleaning the scanner and photo before the actual scan may seem a bit compulsive, but the fact is, if the photo or the scanner's copy glass has dust or dirt on it, that same dust and dirt will be faithfully scanned into the resulting image file. While it is true that this unwanted debris can be removed in the computer, it takes time to do it that way. I did three timing runs with three different photographs with varying amounts of dust, dirt, and dog hair on them. On the average, I was able to remove the debris using Photoshop in about 18 minutes. I then cleaned all three images and the scanners before scanning them in again. It took about 20 seconds to clean the scanner glass and each photo. Hence, it is a true saying that while we never seem to have enough time to do it right, we always find time to correct the mistakes.

I almost hate to include this, but since I know of at least three people who have done it, it bears mention. Don't wipe your photos with moistened towelettes or a cloth treated with dusting products like Pledge or Endust.

Align the Image on the Scanner

Because most photo-editing programs offer the ability to straighten an image that was scanned in crooked, a great temptation is to place the image on the scanner using the edge of the scanner glass as a guide, flop down the lid, and hope for the best. If you will spend a few moments properly aligning the photo on the scanner, you won't need to do it later with the photo-editing program and will have a better scan, since software rotation of any electronic image degrades it. For more about this, see the following sidebar about rotating images with software.

Scanning Near the Edge

Most flatbed scanners today produce excellent scans. Because of the way that the scanning head is mechanically moved along the length of the scanner during a scan, the quality of the scan produced at the very edge of the scanning glass is typically not as good as that produced by the area scanned in the middle of the glass. This is not to say that photos placed near the edge of the scanner glass will be worse that those placed in the middle. It is just a fact that scans made with the photo

Did you know?

Rotating Scanned Images Using Software Degrades Them

3

Anytime an image is rotated using software, it is degraded, with the exception of rotations that are angles of 90°, 180°, or 270°, which do not degrade the image. This is because when the image is rotated at angles other than the ones mentioned, the computer must re-create (called *resample*) every pixel in the image to create the effect of rotation. The most common result of this resampling is a noticeable loss of detail and an overall softening of the photo. Images with a lot of *noise* in them (noise usually appears as tiny specks of bright or dark areas) or scans of printed materials when rotated will develop unwanted checkerboard-like patterns called moiré patterns. The bottom line: it is better to take a few extra minutes to get the image aligned correctly than to attempt to correct it later in software.

positioned away from the edge of the glass will be slightly to noticeably better than those scanned at the edge; how much better is determined by the quality of the scanner. Less expensive scanners do a poorer job of scanning the edge than do higher quality scanners.

Alignment Techniques

So, how do you align a photo placed in the middle of the scanner glass? It depends on what you are scanning. If it is a photograph whose edge is parallel with the border edge, here is a simple technique:

1. Place the plastic right-angle (90° angle) triangle on the scanner glass (as shown in Figure 3-2), and then place the photo on it.

2. After it is aligned, leaving the plastic triangle on the glass, slowly put the lid back down on the scanner. If the image being scanned is very thin and lightweight, be aware that it is very easy for the air flow produced by replacing the lid to move the photo.

3. Make a preview scan. The result is a photo that is aligned with the scanner and that can be selected as shown in Figure 3-2 without cropping off any edges of the photo.

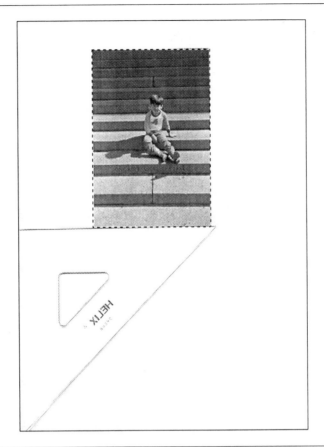

FIGURE 3-2   A plastic triangle provides a quick and accurate way to align a photo on your scanner.

Aligning Images with Crooked Edges

Many times a photo is cut crooked, producing a border that is not parallel with the actual edge of the photograph. This happens most often when multiple photos are printed on a single sheet of paper, and then each photo is cut out using a pair of scissors. To align these properly, we need a sheet of graph paper and some Post-it adhesive.

1. Place a small dab of the restickable adhesive in the middle of a sheet of graph paper. The amount and number of dabs placed on the paper are

3

determined by the size and weight of the photo being scanned. Larger and/or thicker images may require several dabs distributed on the paper.

2. Gently place the photo on top of the adhesive, making only very light contact. (We don't want it to stick yet.)

3. Lay the plastic triangle on top of the photograph so that it is aligned with the lines on the graph paper.

4. Rotate the photo so that the edge of the photograph is aligned with the edge of the triangle as shown next, and then press the photo firmly to set it.

5. Remove the triangle and place the paper face down on the scanner glass with the edge of the paper aligned with the edge of the scanner glass, replace the lid, and scan the photo.

6. When scanning is completed, you can easily remove any adhesive that remains on the back of the photos by balling it up with your fingers.

Exercise caution when applying adhesive to certain materials. For example, old newspaper clippings tend to be very brittle and might be damaged if you attempted to glue them to the graph paper. It has been my experience that alignment is less critical with newspaper clippings, so I recommend using the plastic triangle to align the straightest edge. While most old photographs I have worked with have tended to be thick and stiff, a few heirloom materials can actually be harmed by the light from the scanner. See Chapter 15 for more information about scanning and preserving these types of materials.

Aligning Crooked Photos

If the border is straight but the actual photograph is crooked, you can use the previous technique to straighten out the photograph. The only difference is, at step 4 you must align either a vertical or horizontal element of the photo with the edge of the plastic triangle. Figure 3-3 is an example of three flagpoles that were part of a series of photos taken to get all of the flags blowing out straight from the poles. Unfortunately, the camera was crooked when the photo was taken, so I stuck the photo to some graph paper so that the poles were parallel to the grid, then scanned the image. Figure 3-4 shows the cropping that was done when the photo was selected. A small portion of the photograph will be lost when the photo is scanned, but if it had been rotated using a photo-editing program, the same portion would have been lost. One final detail is the fact that the word "YMCA" on the flag was

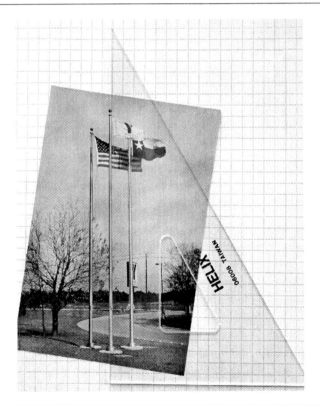

FIGURE 3-3   Even a crooked photograph can be straightened out with your scanner.

FIGURE 3-4   The flagpoles will be straight when scanned into the computer.

backwards. When I scanned it in, I had the scanner apply a horizontal flip to the scanned image, and it resulted in the photo shown in Figure 3-5.

TIP   *After carefully aligning a photo on a scanner and looking at the preview, you may discover that the photo is upside down. Don't reposition the photo, but rather locate the rotate (also called "mirror") function of the scanner and have the scanner flip the image. The scanner can do it with no loss of image quality.*

Steps to a Great Scan

Now that we are ready to scan, we need to start the software that controls the scanner. This can be done one of two ways. You can press a button located on the front of the scanner that launches the scanning software that was put into your computer when you installed the scanner, or you can start the scanner directly from your photo-editing software. In most photo-editing programs, the scanning software

FIGURE 3-5 The scanner even flipped the image so that "YMCA" doesn't read backward.

is launched by choosing the Import command in the File menu (File | Import) and selecting the scanner from a list like the Photoshop Elements example shown in Figure 3-6. Other image-editing software applications (like Jasc's Paint Shop Pro, Corel PHOTO-PAINT, and Collage) launch the interface to the scanner by choosing File | Acquire Image.

When starting the scanner from within another application like Photoshop Elements or Word, avoid using the WIA interface if you can. This interface is a primitive tool that does not use many of the scanner features and will not produce the best possible scanning results.

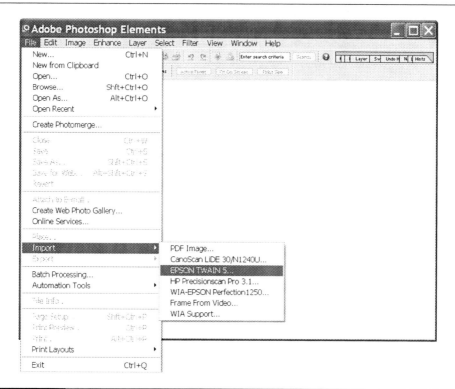

FIGURE 3-6   Starting the scanner from within the photo-editing program

Regardless of how you do it, or which scanner software you are using, the process is still the same. Here are the basic steps to follow to scan an image.

1. Preview the image.

2. Select the image.

3. Choose settings.

4. Scan image.

5. Review scan.

6. Rescan if necessary.

 *Many scanners on the market today start in a fully automatic mode of operation. While it provides a quick and easy way to scan an image, it does not always produce the best scans. For optimum scans, I recommend that you not use the automatic feature.*

Preview the Image You're Scanning

Most scanning software produces a preview image as soon as the scanner is started. In some cases, the preview scan will not occur immediately, because the software is waiting for the lamp in the scanner to warm up, which assures the color accuracy of the scan. In some cases, the scanner may be waiting for you to initiate the preview scan.

Nearly all preview scans are low-resolution representations of the scanned image. Though the preview is a low-quality image, it is used to select the area to be scanned and to verify the color mode setting of the scanner.

Select the Area to Be Scanned (Cropping)

From the preview, you select the area of the scanner glass that you want to scan. Your scanner may attempt to automatically select the image area for you, and most of the time it will do a good job. The two situations where it doesn't work are when the border color of the image being scanned is similar to the color of the inside of the scanner lid and when you want to scan only a part of the image placed on the scanner.

Refine Your Selection with Zooming

When you are selecting a single item out of many on a sheet of paper, or when the selection of the area to be scanned is critical, here is how to make an accurate selection.

1. On the preview, click and drag a rectangle of the area that you want to scan, as shown next. After you have made a rough selection, you can move the selection bars by clicking and dragging them to the desired position.

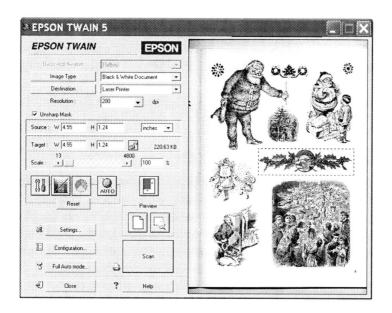

3

2. After you have made the first selection, locate the button or command that zooms in on the selected area. On the Epson dialog box, shown above, it is the button with the magnifying glass in the Preview section. On HP scanners, it is usually a magnifying glass icon. When zoom is enabled, the scanner will scan the image again, and the selected area will fill the preview window, as shown next. At this point, you can make any final adjustments to the selection bars.

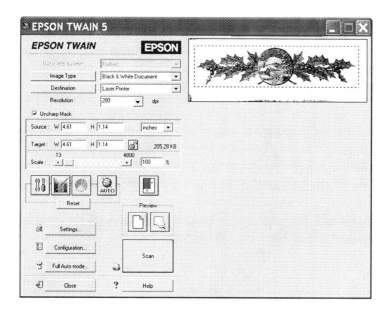

3. If the photo isn't oriented correctly, you can rotate it at this point, or scan it into the computer and rotate it using your photo-editing software. Remember, rotations in multiples of 90° do not degrade image quality.

With the selection the way you want it, you have only a few more checks to make.

Select the Correct Input Mode

Not so long ago, the dialog box that controlled the scanner would ask the user to select the color input mode from choices like line art, halftone, grayscale, 256-color, RGB color, plus all of the possible naming variations of these modes used by different scanner manufacturers. Now the scanner software that you work with will try and determine what kind of image you are scanning and describe the scanner color mode in terms of what the image is. I have found that the more full-featured scanners that cost a little more still tend to describe the mode rather than the type of image being scanned.

The following table illustrates some of the more popular terms used to describe the various color input modes:

Technical Term	Commonly Described As
Line Art	Black-and-white document, OCR (Optical Character Recognition), bitmap (1-bit)
Grayscale	Black-and-white photo, 256 gray shades
Grayscale with de-screening	Black-and-white document
256-color	Web graphics, web palette
RGB color	Color photo, millions of colors
RGB color with de-screening	Color document
48-bit color	Billions of colors

 *Scanning printed material can create moiré patterns, so most scanners offer a feature that eliminates or greatly reduces these patterns. The process is called "de-screening," and it is usually selected automatically by the scanner, depending on your input mode selection.*

As a general rule, the scanning software is pretty accurate in guessing the correct color mode. Here are a few guidelines:

- **Web Color Graphics**   Though they might eventually be converted to 256-color, scan these as RGB color images, since many of the filters and features in your photo-editing software need RGB color images to work.

- **OCR**   If you are scanning pages of printed text to convert them into text files, you will find that the OCR application that does the conversion will also control the scanning.

- **Line Art**   These are black-and-white images that you usually find on business cards. The images have only two colors: black and white. Line art should not be confused with grayscale. If you are scanning line art that is less than pristine, I recommend reading the section in Chapter 9 that discusses this topic in greater detail.

- **48-bit Color**   This mode can only be used if both the scanner and the photo-editing program you are using support it. While it can provide greater detail capture for some images, the files are huge and not recommended unless you are using Photoshop and have a powerful system with lots of memory, a calibrated monitor, and lots of patience.

Quick Solutions for Better Scans

With the selection made and the color mode selected, you are ready to scan. Before you press the scan button, here are some thoughts to consider.

Advantages and Disadvantages of the Automatic Approach to Scanning

Most scanning software does a great job of automatically determining the best settings to get a good scan of the image on the scanner glass. If you have a lot of photographs to scan and you either cannot invest the time, or the quality of the resulting scan isn't critical, you will discover that you can quickly convert a shoebox full of old photos into electronic image files. While writing this book, I have been using an HP 5500C scanner (see Figure 3-7) that has a built-in photo feeder that lets me put in as many as 24 photos and batch feed them. It moves the photos on a cushion of air much like a hovercraft. The time saved over manually putting in the photos one at a time is enormous. The only issue I had with this scanner is that the air system is a little noisy and sounds very much like a small vacuum cleaner.

Because of the way that the automatic scanner features work in adjusting things like exposure and color controls, you will get a good scan most of the time. Photos

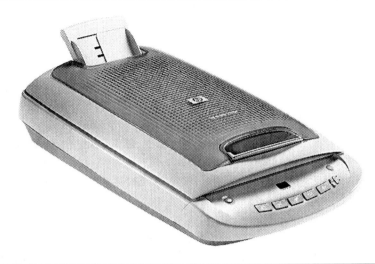

FIGURE 3-7   This HP 5500C scanner provides a quick and easy way to scan in a lot of photos.

that are backlit, color faded, overexposed, and the like will not fare as well as those photos that look great.

Resolution—You Need Less Than You Might Imagine

With scanners offering resolutions of 2400 dots per inch (dpi) or greater, it often surprises users to see that the automatic resolution selection is set for 200 dpi for most types of images. It is commonly believed that increasing the scanning resolution increases the sharpness and clarity of the scanned image, but for most types of scanning it is not true. Increasing the resolution makes the scans take longer and creates huge image files without any visible improvements out of your printer. I strongly recommend that you not change this setting. So, why do scanners offer these super-high resolution values if they are only going to scan at resolutions in the low hundreds? Actually, these higher resolutions are necessary for scanning color slides and negatives, which is covered in Chapter 11, and for making images larger.

Change Image Size (Within Limits)—Scaling

One of the great features of a scanner that is rarely used is the ability to change the size of an image. While this was discussed in Chapter 2, it bears repeating. The physical size of an image can be changed in a photo-editing program through a process called resampling. No matter how good the program is, when you increase the size of a photo this way, the image is visibly degraded in that it loses sharpness and detail. If the original photo is *scaled* by the scanner when it is scanned, it can be made larger without the associated loss of detail. Scaling is accomplished by having the scanner scan at a higher resolution, which produces more pixels and creates a larger picture. Having said that, I would like to interject a saying that is popular here in Texas—You can't make a silk purse out of a sow's ear. If the original photo is of poor quality, the resulting larger image will also be poor quality. And as a result of being larger, the defects will be more apparent.

The best use for scaling is when you are scanning a photo for a particular publication like a newsletter and need a photo that is a specific size for placement. After you have cropped the photo with the selection area, you can tell the scanner what size the output needs to be, and it will do the math and produce a scanned image at the desired size. You can usually either choose the scaling in percentage, or choose the easy way, which is to tell the program what the finished size is supposed to be. The dialog box shown next is the one used in one of the HP scanners.

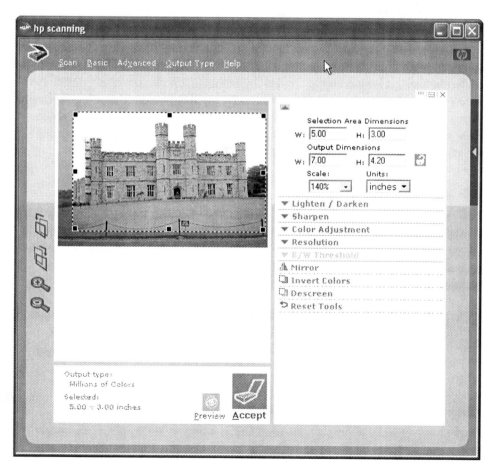

About Keeping Aspect Ratios?

The aspect ratio of an image describes the ratio of picture width to picture height. When defining the area to be scanned, the aspect ratio feature of the scanner software is unlocked by default. This means you can change the ratio of the width to the height of the selection area. Once the image is scanned into an image editing program, the aspect ratio is typically locked to prevent the image from being distorted. The exception to this rule is when you are using the crop tool to change the aspect ratio.

Scan the Image—Finally

The final step is to scan the image. If the scanning software was launched from within a photo-editing application like Paint Shop Pro or Photoshop Elements, the scanned image appears in an image window within the program. If the scanner was started by using a button on the front or by launching the scanning software from the computer, most scanning software will offer you the choice of sending the image to a photo-editing program, printing it, or saving it as a file. In the next chapter, we will learn about the different formats available to save scanned images, and the advantages and disadvantages of each type.

Review the Scan

The last step is to look at the scanned image. The scanning job isn't complete until you have reviewed the scanned image using a photo-editing program. This step is necessary because the image we have been looking at throughout this chapter has been the low-resolution preview image, which doesn't have enough quality to evaluate the scan. Here are some things to look for when evaluating the scan.

> **TIP** *While you can view the scanned image with either the Windows image viewer or your Internet browser (if they were saved as JPEG or GIF images), these viewing tools do not always provide an accurate display of the image.*

Does the Image Have Fingerprints, Dust, or Debris on It?

Foreign objects may appear as tiny blotches of white or black. If you see more than a few, remove the photo and clean it. Verify that the scanner glass is clean, position it back on the scanner glass, and scan it again. If only one or two small dirty defects show, and the scan appears to be otherwise in good shape, it may take less time to use the clone tool of your photo-editing program to remove it, which is covered in Chapter 14.

Does the Scan Appear to Be Crooked?

Though you aligned the photo on the scanner, sometimes replacing the lid has a whoosh effect in which the air being displaced by the lid moves the image ever so slightly. It is worth repeating that even though your image-editing program can correct a crooked scan; it does so at the price of slight image degradation. In addition to this, with most photo editors, getting the correct rotation angle can take as long as or longer than realigning and rescanning the image. Your best response is to remove the photo, realign it, and scan it again.

Is the Image Over or Under Exposed?

The scanner sets its exposure based on the average values of the entire image being scanned, so if, for example, one part of a photo is really overexposed (also called "blown out"), it will affect the scanner's overall exposure settings and produce a darker than desired scan. In Chapter 10, we will learn how to compensate for these problems.

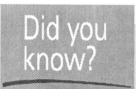

How Zoom Levels Affect What You See

When viewing your scanned image with a photo-editing program or any other image viewer, you need to be aware that bitmap images may appear to have distortion when viewed at zoom levels that are not 100 percent. This is because at zoom levels other than 100 percent, you are not actually viewing the scanned image but rather an approximation of what the computer calculates the image would look like at the selected zoom level. The most common forms of distortion are diagonal lines in an image that may appear to be jagged or the appearance of moiré patterns.

The type of image you are viewing also affects how much distortion may be produced at different zoom levels. For example, a color photo may suffer little to no distortion, whereas a black-and-white (line art) image may appear badly corrupted. In almost all cases, the zoom percentage is displayed somewhere in the title bar of the image window.

Copyright Issues or...
You May Not Own the Picture of You

A word to the wise—just because you can scan it, doesn't mean you can scan it. Sounds sort of Zen doesn't it? I am sure most of you are aware that nearly everything that is in print is copyrighted in one form or another. Most of these cases are obvious. For example, you wouldn't think of scanning a photograph from an issue of *National Geographic* and selling it as desktop wallpaper. You wouldn't—right? While that would be an obvious copyright infringement, others are more subtle.

It is illegal to make copies of any photograph that was made by a professional photographer or studio. Examples of this are school photos and wedding pictures taken by a hired professional—not the cheesy ones taken with the disposable camera during the reception. As strange as it may sound, the law states that although you may have paid a person or organization to take the picture of you or your loved ones and you have paid for the materials, the image still belongs to the photographer or studio, and it is a violation of U.S. copyright law to duplicate them.

Scanning and reproducing bank notes (legal tender), passports, or making extra copies of your payroll check is illegal, so don't do it. It is illegal to OCR scan and reproduce any copyrighted documents—like this book. While we are at it, scanning and copying sheet music is also a copyright infringement. The exception to this is any document that is in the public domain, which might apply to documents created before 1922. Anything created after 1922 pretty much falls under U.S. copyright laws.

Is Your Bible Public Domain or Not?

The King James Version of the Holy Bible is considered public domain. Most of the other popular translations or paraphrases, like the New International Version (NIV), The Living Bible, and so on, are copyrighted and jealously protected by the copyright holders.

Chapter 4

Save What You Have Scanned

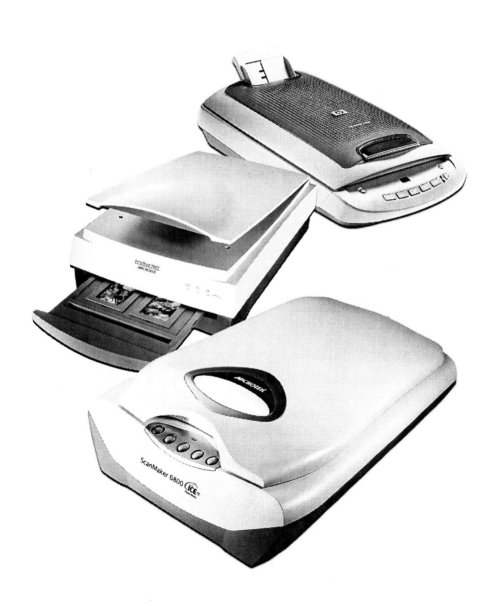

How to...

- ■ Save scanned images
- ■ Select the best graphic format
- ■ Pick the best compression schemes
- ■ Use different storage devices
- ■ Organize your images

After going to all this work to scan an image, you need to save the image. It is usually about this time you are presented with a large assortment of image types with strange sounding names. In this chapter, we will explore several options for saving your scans, and we will learn the trade-offs involved in making large image files as small as possible.

The procedure for saving scanned images isn't complicated and involves the following steps:

1. Select the format for saving the scanned image.

2. Determine the best media for storage or transport.

3. Choose the settings for the selected graphic format.

4. Save the image file.

Types of Graphic Files

The first decision you must make before saving any scanned image is what graphics format to use. The way an image is saved using your scanning software or your photo-editing program is just like saving a letter in your word processor or any other Windows program. What makes it seem complicated is when you notice that you can save the files in many different formats. If you are new to computer graphics, look at the list of graphic formats that a photo-editing program supports, like those in Photoshop Elements, shown in Figure 4-1. Having so many choices can almost take your breath away, yet you will actually need to use only a few formats.

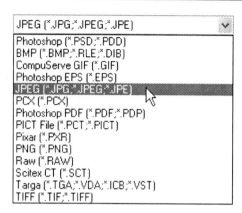

| FIGURE 4-1 | Many different file formats can be used to save images. |

Don't let all of the names of these formats confuse you. Essentially all of the formats can be categorized into one of the following groups:

- **Internet formats**   These formats are used to send with e-mails and post on web pages. They are used because most Internet browsers recognize and display them.

- **Graphic standard formats**   When you need to save the file in a format that someone else can open, you use one of the formats considered industry standards for graphic exchange.

- **Native formats**   When saving files for later use with your own photo editor, you can save the image in a file format that maintains all of the information that is unique to that application, like layers, selections, and so on. Any file format that is unique to the program that saved it is called its *native format.*

Internet Formats

The size of graphic files sent over the Internet must be as small as possible so they can be downloaded quickly. To make the images smaller, some form of compression is applied to the files. The two most popular formats that have built-in file compression are GIF and JPEG (includes JPEG 2000). Two types of compression are used in file formats: the type of compression that reduces file size by roughly 50 percent and preserves the image (called *lossless*) and a compression that achieves a great amount of compression (up to 90 percent) with some image degradation (called *lossy*). Table 4-1 summarizes the differences between the two formats.

When to Use JPEG or GIF

While JPEG is great, it isn't going to replace GIF anytime soon; for some types of images, GIF is the best choice for image quality, file size, or both. To understand when to use JPEG requires that you know which kinds of images work best with it. Overall, JPEG is superior to GIF for storing full-color or grayscale images like scanned photographs, continuous-tone artwork, and similar material. Any scanned image containing smooth variations in color, such as occurs in highlighted or shaded areas, will be represented more accurately and, as importantly, in less space by using JPEG rather than GIF.

GIF does best when you're saving scanned images containing only a few distinct colors, such as simple logos, line drawings, and cartoons. For these types of images, the compression in GIF is not only lossless, but in most cases, it actually compresses them more than JPEG can. This is because large areas of pixels of identical colors are compressed more efficiently by GIF. JPEG can't compress this type of data as much as GIF does without introducing artifacts.

	GIF	JPEG
Compression	**Lossless** Fixed amount of compression applied. No loss of image quality	**Lossy** User selects the amount of compression. Some loss of image quality, depending on amount of compression applied
Compression Results	Moderate file size reduction	Greatly reduced file size
Color Depth	Can only be used on 256-color images	Can be used on 24-bit color or grayscale images
Best used with	Low-color cartoon-like images, line drawings, and logos	All photographs
Allows transparency giving the appearance of seeing through an image or of an image floating on a background	Yes	No

TABLE 4-1 Comparison Between JPEG and GIF File Formats

Graphic Standard Formats

When you need to send a scanned image to a printer or a service bureau, they will most likely ask for it in a graphics format that has become the de facto standard for publishing. Its official name is Tagged Image Format File, but everyone refers to it by its initials, *TIFF* or *TIF.* TIFF files also offer several lossless compression options, but as with the GIF files, you can only expect a 40 percent to 50 percent reduction in file size. Newer versions of photo editors offer the ability to save an image as a TIFF file using JPEG compression. Be aware that many older photo-editing programs cannot read these files.

4

> TIP
>
> *Many professionals use a format called "Encapsulated PostScript" (EPS). This format is the choice of many graphics professionals for sending graphic art to a printer or service bureau, because it is the ideal format for saving vector data. While this format can be used for bitmap files of photographic images, it wasn't really designed for it, and the resulting EPS file size can become very large—very, very large.*

Another format that is used a lot in the Windows environment is BMP. When you want to save a scanned image for use as wallpaper on your Windows platform, you should save it as a BMP file.

> TIP
>
> *To preserve the quality of scanned images that are important or require photo editing, you should always save a copy using one of the non-lossy formats like TIFF.*

Native Formats

While scanning software does not have a native format, you can save a file in your photo-editing program's native format and open it later without any loss of special features or information that can only be interpreted and used by that program. This is the format of choice for important images that you may want to revisit at a later date. Why not save all of the images in native format? First of all, the files can get quite large, especially if the image contains lots of layers. Secondly, few people have the software necessary to open the file.

Saving your scanned images in any format other than those already mentioned should only be done if you have a specific request for them; otherwise, don't use them.

Saving Options

Depending on the file format you have selected, you may be presented with several more options to choose from when you save a scanned image. Most of the options involve picking a level of compression for JPEG images or choosing a type of compression for TIFF files.

Picking the Best JPEG Compression

Selecting the best JPEG compression is a balancing act between file size and quality. To make things just a little more complicated, it is difficult to predict how much compression can be applied to an image without producing *artifacts,* serious areas of distortion in the image. Also, the settings usually refer to image quality rather than the amount of compression, so a maximum setting means that the selected compression produces the best image and also the largest file. A minimum setting applies maximum compression resulting in the smallest file and the greatest amount of distortion. The setting dialog box for Adobe Photoshop Elements 2.0 is shown here:

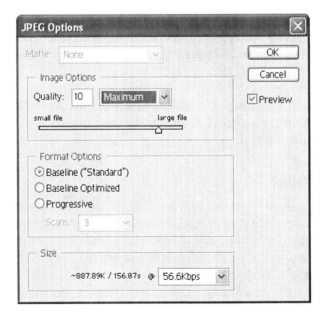

As if all of that weren't enough, the terminology used to describe the quality/ compression setting varies between manufacturers. Figure 4-2 shows two images that were saved as JPEG files at different compression levels. The image on the left was saved at a maximum setting and resulted in a file that was a little over 2MB. The image on the right was saved at minimum image quality and resulted in a 116KB file, but with the artifacts shown.

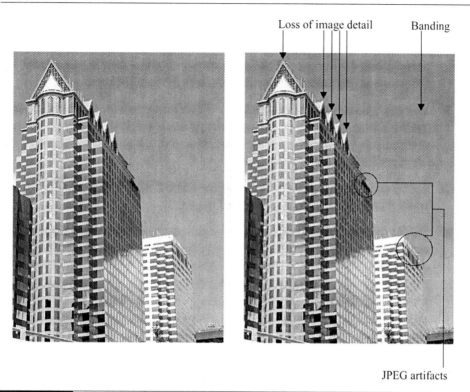

FIGURE 4-2   Comparing the effects of compression maximum quality (left) and
minimum file size (right)

Now that we have covered the basics about JPEG compression, you need to be
aware of some factors that affect the resulting image size and the distortion.

- **Image size**   Stated simply, the larger the image, the less distortion will be
  seen in the resulting file. The original image in Figure 4-2 was very large,
  and when minimum quality/maximum JPEG compression was applied to it,
  almost no distortion could be seen. Not until I resized both images to make
  them small enough to be placed on the Web did the application of maximum
  compression produce the artifacts shown.

- **Image detail**   The amount of detail in an image determines how small
  the resulting file will be. A complex image with lots of contrast will not
  compress nearly as much as a landscape with a large amount of solid blue
  sky in it.

- **JPEG degradation occurs with every save** Each time a JPEG image is opened, modified, and saved, a small amount of loss occurs. Just opening the image to view it doesn't cause any degradation. To put things into perspective, the number of times necessary to open, modify, and save a file to produce noticeable artifacts is from 50 to 200 times.

- **You can't undo compression effects** If an image was saved at a minimum quality setting, a certain amount of damage has been done. Saving this same scanned image at a maximum quality setting will not undo what occurred the first time it was saved.

- **A 256-color image cannot be saved as a JPEG file** JPEG can only be applied to RGB color and grayscale images.

- **Too little compression expands file size** A little-known fact about JPEG compression is that if you apply the maximum quality/lowest compression setting, it actually doubles the image file size rather than compressing it. For example, in Photoshop Elements when you select the maximum quality setting from the pop-up menu, the dialog box displays a setting of 10 (out of a range of 12). If you manually change the quality value to 12, the file size doubles.

- **Solid borders can cause problems** Other little-known facts about JPEG compression are that if your scanned image has a large single-color border around it, it will increase the resulting file size, and the sharp border boundary can create visible artifacts (ghost edges).

Choosing TIFF Compression

As mentioned earlier, compression available for TIFF images is lossless. Despite this, many printers, service bureaus, and other graphic organizations (including the graphics department of my publisher) insist that no compression be applied to TIFF images sent to them. The resulting files can be quite large, but they load very quickly since the file doesn't need to be decompressed before it is opened in an application. To keep your files smaller, I always recommend selecting a compression for the TIFF files; any of the choices will work. The image that follows shows some of the choices available when saving a TIFF file with Photoshop Elements. Two of the choices—Zip and JPEG—are not supported in older programs that can read TIFF files. LZW compression is probably the one most commonly used for TIFF compression on PCs.

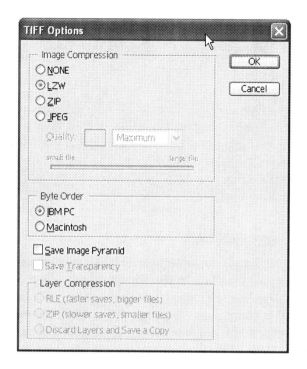

4

We're almost done. You may also have the option to save the color profile associated with the image. While some of the more expensive scanners attach a color profile to the scanned image they produce, the option to attach a color profile to an image file is most often seen in photo-editing programs. This is helpful when the photo will be reproduced by a system that can utilize the color profiles. They are not magic; assigning a profile does not make the colors accurate, it just provides specific parameters to help a color management system produce accurate colors. If you have layers on your image and the file format you selected supports them, then you will have the option of saving the layer information with the image.

You still aren't done yet if the file format you picked has additional options.

TIP *The new photo-editing programs support and save their images in the latest TIFF format. Make sure those who are receiving your scanned images as TIFF files for printing can support the latest version as well, or they may not be able to open your files.*

What Is a Color Profile, Anyhow?

A *color profile* describes how the colors in a device such as a scanner, printer, or monitor map to a particular color space. In other words, it is information that is attached to an image that tells the device reading the file how the colors should be displayed so that they match the colors as they appeared on the system that created the file.

File Format Suggestions

If you are working on images that must be maintained and possibly revisited at a later date, always save the file in native format. For sending to the printer or for placement in a page layout program, save a copy as a TIFF file. If you want to share photos with a friend, save a copy as a JPEG file. Even though it is a lossy compression, the effects of it are only visible when you apply a ridiculously high compression. Some of the newer scanners and photo-editing programs offer the option to save the image as a JPEG 2000 (JP2). This permits greater compression than JPEG, with less image degradation. Before you get all excited and begin to save images in this format, I recommend that you wait until most of the major Internet browsers support this new JPEG standard. If you don't, I promise that you will discover that many of your friends and associates cannot open or view the file. It's a great new standard, but it's still pretty new.

Where Will You Store Your Images?

If you are just scanning a single photo for attachment to an e-mail, you are best served saving the image in the My Photos folder in Windows or in some other folder you create if you are using an earlier version of Windows. If you are archiving a lot of photos, you must be aware that color photos take up a lot of space on the hard drive, so a little prior planning will be beneficial in the long run. Before discussing image management, let's consider the options available for storing your scanned images.

Using Hard Drive Storage

There are two general storage classifications for scanned images—removable and fixed. Fixed storage is generally limited to hard drives, which now come in monster capacities with up to 250 gigabytes (GB), or 250 billion bytes of data, like the one shown here. In fact, there will soon be 350+ GB drives. If you were to store 5×7 color photos scanned at a high resolution and saved as TIFF files on such a drive, the drive could contain 250,000 of them. The advantage of storing your scanned images on hard drives is that the drives are fast and cheap. The primary disadvantage of hard drives is that they are mechanical devices that can and do fail. If you store your photos or other documents on a hard drive, I strongly recommend setting up a duplicate drive to maintain a mirror copy of what is on the drive. My drive is currently holding over 25,000 photos and other documents representing over 30 years of photography and hundreds of hours of scanning both film and photographs. For less than $100 I bought a hard drive sufficient to back up the primary hard drive, and I have set it to back up the primary drive automatically every evening.

Using Removable Storage

When the first IBM PC appeared, it offered only one form of removable media—cassette tape. I am not kidding. The 1.44MB of a traditional floppy disk seems minuscule by today's standards, where over 4 gigabytes can be easily transported to and from work on a single DVD the size of a CD. Now you have so many choices for removable media, it would be impossible to list them all. So the following table lists the more popular forms and even a few that are no longer with us.

Device	Capacity	Comments
3.5" floppy disk	1.44MB	Once the king of portable storage, it is slowly being replaced by the CD recorder. Media cost is very cheap—bordering on free (with rebates).
Zip drive	100–750MB	Still a popular media in the 100MB capacity, although the 250MB and 750MB disks never became as popular as the 100MB. Cost per disk is $8–$10 for 100MB and $12–$18 for the 250MB and 750MB disks.
Memory devices	16MB to 1GB	CompactFlash, SmartMedia, MemoryStick, and the Microdrive are generally used in digital devices like cameras and MP3 players, but they can also be used to store and transport data.
SuperDrive	100MB	No longer sold in the United States. Great idea that entered the market too late. It was popular with many because it could read both regular 3.5" floppy disks and the higher-capacity disk.
CD-Recorder	600–700MB	Called *CD (CDR) burners,* this class of storage device has become the dominant player in the removable media market. With a large capacity and very inexpensive media, it has quickly become the removable media of choice.
Jaz drive	1–2GB	Once the king of high-capacity removable storage, Iomega's now-discontinued Jaz drives were slowly pushed out of the marketplace by faster and cheaper CD burners.
DVD	4.7GB	Slowed by conflicting formats and initially high prices for both the burners and media, the DVD is only now gaining popularity as a mass storage device.

How to Organize Your Images

As your library begins to grow, you will discover that it can be almost as difficult to locate a particular photo file as it is to find a photo stuffed away in a shoebox. If you are a serious amateur or a professional photographer, you need a product that can let you assign keywords, keep track of photos on CDs and in other locations, and that can offer other database management features as well. Several products are out there. I currently am managing a library of over 25,000 photos. (Many of them are poor photos—but my drives are *huge,* so I rarely throw any of my scanned photos away.)

Photo organizers range from really poor shareware to some excellent products such as Jasc Paint Shop Album, Adobe Photoshop Album, Canto Cumulus, and Portfolio by Extensis. The most important feature you should look for in an image manager is how easy it is to set up and use. Other important features are the ability to extract keyword information from existing files and the ability to search by both keywords and thumbnails. Portfolio 6 is an example of a photo organizer (see Figure 4-3). The newer photo organizers go beyond just providing tools to maintain a visual database; they now offer basic image editing and enhancement plus the ability to create cool projects like photo calendars, greeting cards and more. Chapter 12 covers this topic in detail.

4

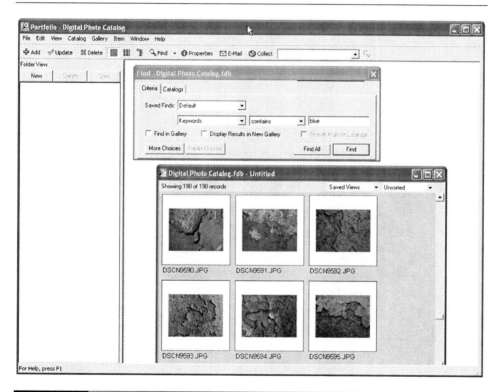

FIGURE 4-3   Portfolio helps me manage a very large image library.

Most of these image managers offer a free 30-day evaluation version of their product, so download one and see if it works for you.

We covered a lot of territory in this chapter, and I hope that you will now give some serious thought to the saving and organization of your image library. Now that you know how to save the images, let's move on to the next chapter and learn about printing all of this stuff that we have scanned.

Chapter 5

Print What You Have Scanned

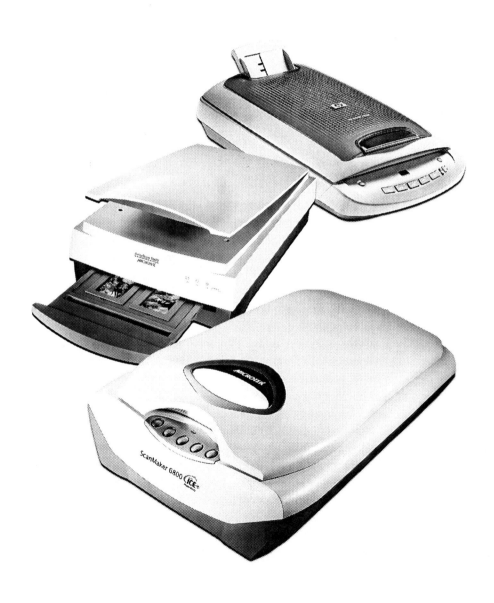

How to...

- Select the best printer for the job
- Understand the difference between photo and non-photo printers
- Maintain and operate your printer
- Match the media to the project

Now that we have scanned and stored the images, many of us want to print the images either for mounting in a scrapbook or as copies to send to friends or family. A few years ago, this would have required a $10,000 printer to get a decent-looking color photograph. Now, with an inkjet printer (costing less than a few hundred dollars) and the new photo papers available, we can produce photographs that look like the real thing.

A Brief History of Consumer Printers

In the beginning there were dot-matrix printers, and all of us playing with computers in those days looked upon the tiny dots and said it was cool—and noisy. Laser printers appeared soon afterward, and while the output (300 dpi) was dazzling, so was the price (over $3,000), so we kept our dot-matrix printers. There was no color in those days.

When inkjet printers first appeared, they only printed black and white, but their output looked like that of the laser printers that we could not afford. I bought one of the first HP inkjet printers, paying over $600 (and that was wholesale). It printed about one page per minute—if I was lucky. The only argument against the inkjet printer when they first appeared was that the ink could smear if the paper got wet. In a short time, the inkjet printers replaced the dot-matrix units, and our collective hearing began to return. Now it was lasers vs. inkjets, but there was still no color. When the first color inkjet printers began to appear on the shelves, they printed color that reminded me of early color TVs back in the 1950s, which produced weird colors, but we didn't care because it was color. In less than three years, the color inkjet printers began to get their collective act together and to produce vivid colors at speeds that rivaled the laser printers. Today you can get an excellent color inkjet printer for less than $150, and few consumer laser printers remain. The price of color laser printers continues to drop, but they are still too expensive for the consumer market because they still cost well over $1,200. Most of the black-and-white laser printers today are found working as high-speed network printers of small companies and large corporations.

Sort Out Today's Available Color Printers

With color inkjet printers being the dominant printer on the market today, you can walk into any office-supply or computer store and see a long line of them on the shelves. Most printer manufacturers offer at least five different models of printers ranging in price from $100 to $800. If that's not confusing enough, if you look at the sample output produced by each printer, it appears that they all have roughly the same quality of output. To help simplify choosing a printer, you need to understand the different printer classifications and what they do. The following are the general categories of color printers available in the marketplace today:

- Color inkjet printers

- Photo inkjet printers—dye-based inks

- Photo inkjet printers—pigment-based inks

- Dye-sublimation printers

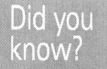

Higher Resolution Doesn't Mean Better Photos

Many inkjet printer manufacturers focus on the printing resolution of their products. Resolutions like 2,400 dots per inch (dpi) are common, with some companies advertising resolutions as high as 5,760 dpi. While these astronomical numbers sound like they will produce the best possible photos, most of them print the stunning sample photos you see in the stores at a resolution of 720 dpi. So what happens if you print one of your photos at a higher resolution like 2,440 dpi? It will take almost four times as long to print the photo and will use twice as much ink, and the worst part is that the shadow areas of the photo may actually appear darker, causing loss of detail. You might wonder then what the higher resolution of the printer is used for. When printing photos that are 8×10 or larger, the higher resolution improves the fine detail in an image. But for smaller photo formats like 5×7 or 4×6, stay with 720 dpi. The bottom line is, when looking for a printer, ignore the resolution figures as a deciding factor as to which printer to buy. When printing a photo, don't be tempted to override the factory recommendations for printing at a lower (720 dpi) resolution.

What Color Inkjet Printers Are All About

Most of the inkjet printers on the market today are color inkjet printers. Most print their color using a black ink cartridge and a color cartridge containing three different-colored inks (called a *tri-color cartridge*). Black is always maintained as a separate color for two reasons: it allows the printing of standard text without wasting any color, and secondly, while it is theoretically possible to create black using the three different-colored inks together, in fact the color produced looks more like dark mud than black. Color inkjet printers offer very fast print speeds (for text); some can print on both sides of the paper (duplex). HP has a printer that can detect what kind of paper is in your printer and automatically select the correct media settings. In short, they are pretty amazing.

What a Dye-Based Photo Inkjet Printer Is Best For

Almost every photo inkjet printer that you can find prints using dye-based inks. In the next section, we will learn a little more about pigment-based ink printers, but for now, let's understand what makes a color inkjet different from a photo inkjet printer.

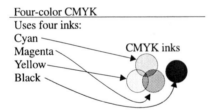

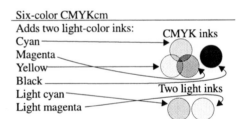

Most color inkjet printers are described as four-color printers in that they use four inks to produce color output. The four inks used are black (K), cyan, magenta, and yellow (CMY). Some three-color printers on the market still create their color output using CMY, and they have a separate black pigment–based ink cartridge that is only used for printing text. Three-color printers do not produce good color, especially for photos, and should be avoided.

Photo inkjet printers are six-color printers that use black (K), cyan, light cyan, magenta, light magenta, and yellow (CcMmY), which allows the printer to print a much greater range of colors than would be possible with only a CMY color cartridge. Your average photo printer has a black cartridge and either a six-color cartridge or another configuration that has been gaining popularity, a black cartridge and a tri-color cartridge that can be replaced with a six-color cartridge. That said, the

Did you know?

Do You Know the Color Symbols?

The major colors used in printing have single-letter abbreviations. Most of these color abbreviations make sense, for example, the primary colors are red (R), green (G), and blue (B); the complementary colors are cyan (C), magenta (M), and yellow (Y). Then there is black (K), whose abbreviation you might expect to be *B,* but that letter is already used by blue. There are also two light versions of the colors, light cyan (c) and light magenta (m), which are used in six-color printers. These are referred to as *light colors,* not because they have half the calories of regular colors, but because they have half of the color content of the regular color.

difference in the output between the six-color and the four-color is subtle, not a jaw-dropping kind of difference. To add to the confusion, many photo printers look identical to the color printer model made by the same manufacturer, because they only differ in the print-head mechanicals and the internal electronics needed for the additional colors.

Which should you buy? Since the photo printers are dedicated primarily to printing photos, they are traditionally slower at printing text documents than the regular color printer. If a majority of what you are printing is photos, then you should get a photo printer. But if you only print photos occasionally, then a standard desktop color printer is your best bet. The color photos printed by these wonders are so close to the output of a photo printer that you need to do a side-by-side comparison to see any difference in the output in most cases.

Why Print Longevity Matters

After you have printed a photo, a legitimate concern should be how long the photo will last before it fades. Now that most of the photo printers can print photos that look just like the regular photographs we have come to know and love, the printer manufacturers have started to deal with a real-world fact that dye-based inks tend to fade over time. Most dye-based prints are fade resistant for between 5 and 25 years, depending on where they are stored and the type of media used.

The solution to the fading problem was to create a pigment-based ink printer that produces a photograph that will not fade for a long time. Epson made just such a printer a few years ago called a Stylus Photo 2000P. Its pigment-based inks could produce a photograph that was resistant to fading for over 100 years. They even have archival ink they claim won't fade for 200 years. This longevity is great for archival reasons, but the colors of the pigment-based inks are not as vivid as those produced by dye-based inks. Epson went back to the drawing board and produced the next generation of this printer, the Stylus Photo 2200. While it is still a pigment-based ink printer, they are able to create a vivid color output that is very close to that of a dye-based ink printer. So why don't all of the printer manufacturers switch over to pigment-based inks? Cost is the main reason. The Epson Stylus Photo 2200, shown in Figure 5-1, sells for six times as much as a regular dye-based photo printer.

Who Needs Print Longevity?

Professional photographers who are selling their photographs to clients need to be able to deliver a photo that will stand the test of time. Cost is not an issue since it is factored into what they charge you for the print. If you are not a professional photographer or feel that $700–$800 is more money than your budget can handle, I have good news for you. Consider the photo that you just scanned in and printed on your photo printer. What if it does begin to fade after five years? Print another copy. The only difference is that in five years the new photo printer models will produce even better output and will probably be cheaper than they are now.

FIGURE 5-1   The Epson Stylus Photo 2200 produces photos that will last longer than you will.

What a Dye-Sublimation Printer Is Best For

Now that we have explored dye-based and pigment-based inks, it is time to look at the type of printer that arguably makes the best color. Dye-sublimation ("dye-sub") printers produce outstanding color. This was, and still is, the type of printer used to test for color accuracy of printed output by professional printers. Until a few years ago, the cheapest dye-sub printer you could buy was in the neighborhood of $15,000. Now, several companies make small dedicated dye-sub photo printers that produce photos that look just like the ones from photo developers. The one I use is the Sony DPP-SV77 photo printer (see Figure 5-2). Selling for around $300, its color is stunning, because dye-sub printers actually produce a continuous-tone output like real film. If my Sony printer has a limitation, it is that the maximum size of the prints it can produce is 4×6", which suits about 90 percent of my needs. Larger dye-sub printers are also available that are significantly more expensive than the equivalent inkjet printer.

As good as dye-sub printers are, the cost per print is relatively high. This is because of the way that dye-sub printers work. They have an internal coated ribbon consisting of CMYK color inks that are transferred to the image. Each photo you print uses a complete set of the four sheets of different colors (CMYK) regardless

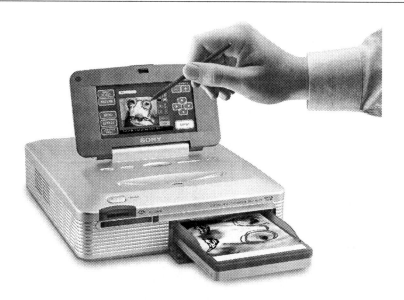

FIGURE 5-2   The Sony DPP-SV77 photo printer is a dye-sub printer that produces stunning color photographs.

of the color content of the image. For example, if I were to print a photo of a single tiny red square in the middle of a white field, it would consume the same amount of color ribbon as a photo of a grand display of flowers. My little Sony probably costs me about 48¢ per print. When you consider I can take a CD down to my local one-hour photo lab and get the same size print for around 25¢ per copy, you can see that you are paying for convenience.

What You Need to Know About Printer Ink and Media

It is a poorly kept secret that printer manufacturers make very little profit on the printers that they sell and look to the sale of the consumables (ink and paper) to make the profits that keep shareowners happy. Because these consumables are so expensive, many third-party companies provide their own ink cartridges and refill kits for existing cartridges, while others make photo papers.

Should You Use Those Third-Party Ink Cartridges?

The important question is, are the inks used by the third-party ink cartridge vendors as good as those provided by the manufacturer? I have tested several of them and found that the quality of their output ranges from poor to good. My recommendation is to use the printer manufacturer's cartridges if you only use a few cartridges each year. If your cartridge demands are heavier than that, you may want to consider one of the zillion vendors on the Internet. The only way to find out how good a third-party replacement cartridge is, is to first print a sample photo using the printer manufacturer's cartridges and then to buy a set, print another sample, and compare the results you get with their product. If you are not satisfied with the results, return the cartridges and ask for a refund. If you are satisfied with them, continue to use them and occasionally print another sample print, because the quality assurance of some of these houses varies.

Use the Media that Produces the Best Results for You

It used to be that paper was just paper; now it is a specialized media. Each type of paper is made for a specific purpose—inkjet paper, photo paper, photo glossy paper, and so on, and those are just the ones that you see at the retail stores. Many more unusual types of inkjet papers are available on the Internet. I have seen papers to turn photos into puzzles, or to put a photo on a coffee cup, or even to put them on a canvas. There are a lot of specialty papers out there so I thought we should cover a few general facts about inkjet papers before we finish this chapter.

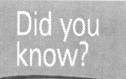

What's at Stake if You Use Third-Party Inkjet Cartridges?

Most printer manufacturers state that using these third-party ink supplies voids the printer's warranty. Most users believe this. Manufacturers have threatened in the past to void printer warranties when cartridges are refilled. The brand of supplies you purchase for your printer is your decision. You are *not* required by any machine manufacturer's warranty to use only its brand. The Magnuson-Moss Warranty Improvement Act prevents manufacturers from doing that.

5

Printing color photos on cheap copy paper produces poor pictures even though it uses the same amount of ink as printing on photo paper. Printing a lousy- looking photo on a very expensive paper won't make the photo look any better. The secret to getting the best results printing your scanned images is to find a paper that has the texture and finish that you like and then to experiment with your printer settings to get the results that you want.

Adjust Your Printer Settings for Best Results

Regardless of which printer you are using, you access the software that controls your printer when you select File | Print in the scanner software or photo-editing application. The dialog box shown next is from Photoshop Elements 2.0. The printer that is selected is an Epson Stylus Photo 780 printer.

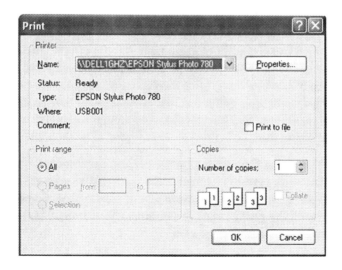

While the specific details will vary from printer to printer, the procedure described next works for most situations.

1.   When selecting a printer, you'll see a properties button alongside the printer name. Clicking the button launches the printer-specific software, like the one shown next, which allows you to control many of the printer features.

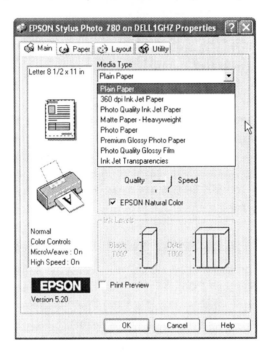

2.   Within the printer dialog box you can select the media that is loaded in the printer as well as the color management that the printer should use to print the scanned image. The choices of media (paper) are limited to the names and types offered by the printer manufacturer, which can cause a little bit of head scratching when you are using a paper that is different from the choices shown. See the sidebar about matching paper to printers for information on this.

3.   If this is your first time setting up the printer, I recommend that you experiment with several different settings. Print the scanned image and write on the back of the photo what settings were used. Once you are satisfied with the results, save the settings with a unique name, and use these settings to print your photos.

You Should Match Photo Papers with Printer Settings

What happens if you have an Epson photo printer loaded with Kodak photo paper? Looking at the paper pop-up menu, you will not see anything but Epson papers listed. Which Epson paper matches the Kodak paper that you have? The first place to get the answer to this question is the printed information that came with the paper. Most of the paper vendors list the best paper settings for most of the major printer manufacturers. If your printer is too new to be listed, check the paper manufacturer's web site to see if they give setting recommendations for your printer. If both of these don't pan out, try to match the type of paper (glossy, matte, and so on) with one that's close on the printer's paper list.

That just about covers printers with regard to printing photos. In the next chapter, we will become more application specific, beginning with scanning photos and other things intended for display on the Web.

5

Part II

Put Your Scanner to Work

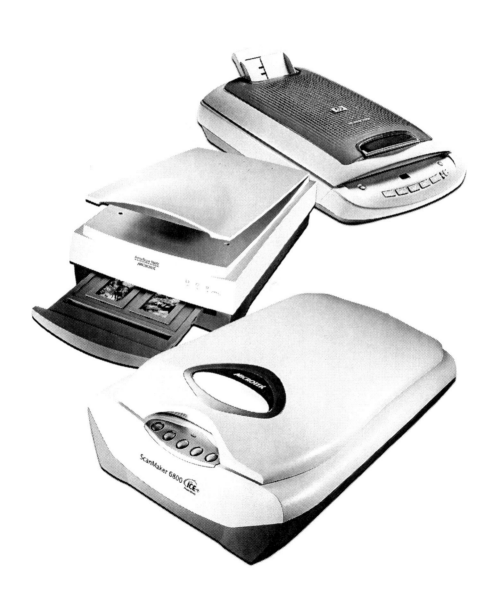

Chapter 6

Scan Graphics for Use on the Web

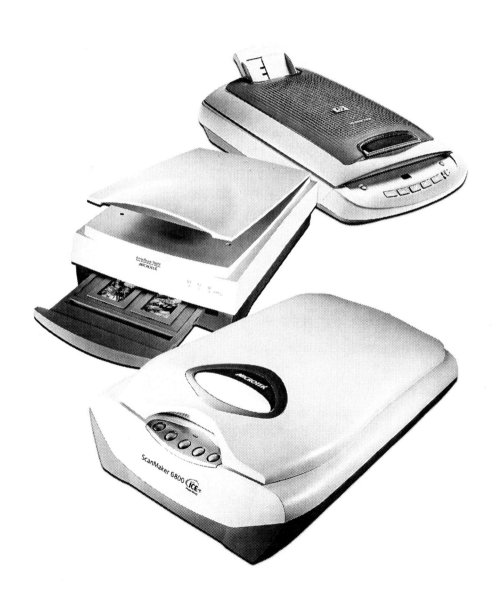

How to...

■ Pick the best size and color mode for the Web

■ Scan and send a photo with an e-mail

■ Scan an image for placement in a web-based photo service

My first experience with the Internet was a long, long time ago, and it was a slow, painful, and very text-oriented one. In those days e-mail was practically unknown, whereas today it has become an integral part of our daily life. I talk to people every day who want to send photographs to friends but don't know how to do it. In this chapter, you will learn how to scan a photograph so it will "fit" into an e-mail (there are size limits) and see the different manual methods for adding the photo to your e-mail. You will also learn how to use several automated methods using either a photo editor (like Photoshop Elements) or the software that was installed with your scanner.

Send a Photo with an E-mail

Let's first learn how to scan and attach a photo to an e-mail the old-fashioned way. The procedure is not complicated, and it involves the following steps:

1. Scan the photo to the correct size.

2. Save it in the best Internet format.

3. Attach the scanned image to an e-mail.

Scan the Photo

The first step involves scanning the photograph into the computer. The first few steps will recap what we learned back in Chapter 3:

1. Ensure the scanner and the photo are clean.

2. Align the photo on the scanner glass, and gently put the lid down.

3. Using the button on the front of the scanner, or from the scanning software, create a preview of the photo as shown next. From this point on, how you scan the image becomes scanner specific, so I have outlined the procedure

in the sections that follow for some of the more popular scanners on the market today.

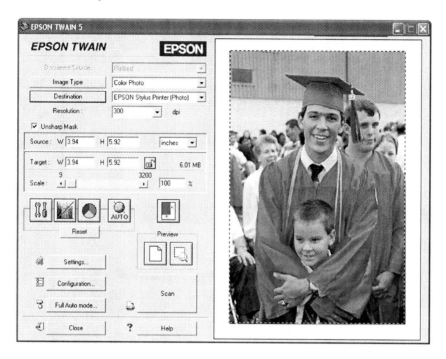

Scan a Photo for E-mail Using an Epson Scanner

While all scanners work fundamentally the same, there are some interesting differences in both nomenclature and procedures when using the Twain software for the Epson scanners. Here is the step-by-step procedure for scanning a photo that will be attached to an e-mail:

1. Change the destination/output setting to Screen/Web. Figure 6-1 shows the dialog box for this, where we change the destination of the scan. Notice that when the Screen/Web setting is changed, the resolution of the scan changes from its original setting of 300 dpi to 96 dpi. Click OK.

2. Click the Scan button and the image is scanned. Epson allows you to continue scanning more images until you are finished.

3. At this point, you will see all of the images in their Image Gallery. If you save them using their factory default settings, they will be saved as BMP files. I recommend using File | Save As and saving the images as JPEG files.

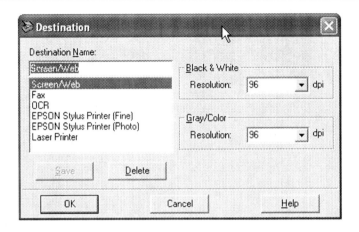

FIGURE 6-1 Change the destination from printer to Screen/Web using Epson's software.

TIP *When a scan is saved by any scanning program, note where the image files are being saved. It will save you a lot of time hunting for them later.*

Did you know?

What Is the Best Image Format for the Web?

The two most commonly used formats for web publishing are GIF and JPEG. The GIF format is limited to a maximum of 256 colors and should only be used for simple graphics like buttons, logos, or icons.

Scanned photographs (either color or grayscale), should be saved as JPEG files. JPEG is capable of reproducing millions of colors or tones, and more importantly, JPEG files can be compressed, which allows you to create a reasonable file size from a fairly large original print. Photos saved using the GIF format may suffer from the limited color palette, and the file size of a color photo in GIF will almost always be larger than the same photo in compressed JPEG format even though it contains fewer colors.

Scan a Photo for E-mail Using an HP Scanner

When scanning a photo using an HP scanner, you will probably use their PrecisionScan Pro software or a newer, more automated version (discussed later in this chapter) that ships with some of their latest scanners. With PrecisionScan Pro, the default choices for images destined for the Internet use a 256-color scan, which needs to be changed to True Color as shown in Figure 6-2.

While 256-color does work, it isn't my first choice for two reasons. The color photo image may be degraded by the conversion to 256 colors, and you cannot manipulate images using a photo editor like Photoshop Elements without converting the scanned photo back to 24-bit color. Therefore, I recommend the following:

6

1. Keep the True Color (16.7 million colors) setting that was probably detected automatically.

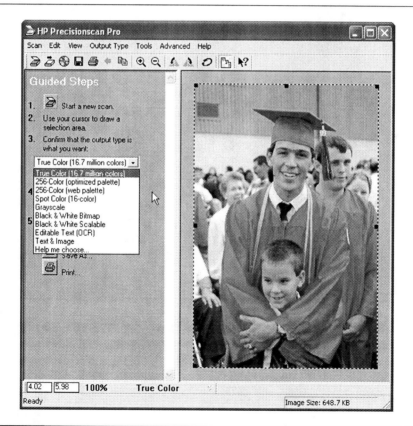

| FIGURE 6-2 | HP's PrecisionScan Pro software wants to use 256-color for web images. |

2. Choose Tools | Change Resolution and change the setting to **96** (dpi) as shown next. You will see that 96 is not one of the preset resolution settings, and you will need to enter it as shown. For more information about the use of 96 dpi, see the sidebar "What's the Best Internet Resolution?" later in this chapter. Please note that when you change the resolution, the file size shown in the lower-right corner of the dialog box changes to reflect the change in resolution. Though this may appear to be a large file size, when it is compressed as a JPEG file, it will become quite small.

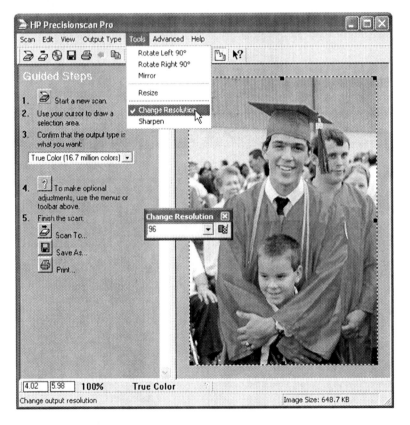

3. Scan the image and save the completed scan. For Windows, you have several choices. The HP software automatically assumes that you want to save the photo as a Windows Bitmap file (*.BMP), and while this will work, for e-mail I recommend that you save it as a JPEG (*.JPEG) file because it compresses the resulting image much smaller.

Scan a Photo for E-mail Using a Canon Scanner

Scanning a photo with a Canon scanner using ScanGear CS gives essentially the same options as found in the HP PrecisionScan Pro. In the advanced dialog box shown in Figure 6-3, choose Color (photo) and change the Output Resolution to **96**. You will see that 96 is not one of the preset resolution settings, and you will need to enter it. For more information about the use of 96 dpi, see the sidebar "What's the Best Internet Resolution?"

Work with Different Photo File Sizes and Resolutions

Since the resolution at which you scan a photo determines its file size and the file size determines how long it will take someone to download the file, the question

6

FIGURE 6-3   Cannon's ScanGear software settings for web-bound color photos

What's the Best Internet Resolution?

When resizing images for viewing on the Internet, you have many traditions and urban myths to deal with. The first is that only 72 dpi will produce the optimum display of a photo on a monitor. Many believe it is true because the computer monitor is 72 pixels per inch (ppi). Surprise, it's not. Apple was the first to use 72 dpi as a screen resolution on the first Macs. It was chosen because it related to the printing standard of 72 points to an inch more than anything else. Others may say that you must scan images at 96 dpi (which is really 96 ppi), because that resolution matches the screen resolution of most computer monitors today. Again, that is not true in most cases. So what's the best resolution? The one that produces a screen image of the scanned photo that fits comfortably in an average computer display set to 800×600. As a general rule, if you scan a standard 4×6" photo at a resolution of 100 dpi, it will fit nicely in most computer monitors at a view magnification level of 100 percent.

you'll want to ask is: What is a reasonable file size for photos that will be attached to an e-mail? No hard-and-fast rules apply, but a good rule of thumb is to keep your total image size no more than 100 to 120 kilobytes (KB). Even if you have one of the new extremely fast broadband cable or DSL Internet connections, remember that many of the people to whom you are sending a photo still move at the much slower pace of 14.4 kilobits per second (Kbps) or 28.8 Kbps phone modems. Approximate download times for a 100K JPEG file are

14.4 Kbps modem—56 seconds
28.8 Kbps modem—28 seconds
56 Kbps modem—14 seconds

Having an image whose file size is too great presents other disadvantages. Many Internet service providers (ISPs) won't accept an e-mail with really large attached files. My ISP draws the line at 5MB. If someone sends me an e-mail with a 6MB file attached, it will be refused before I ever see it. If you scan in a photo that is several megabytes in size and attach it to an e-mail to someone with a slow dial-up modem, in most cases they must wait for your attached photo to download no matter how long it takes. I remember back when I had a 28.8 Kbps modem and someone sent me a 3MB image. Downloading it tied up my computer for 25 minutes—and it was the wrong image!

Did you know?

The Benefits of Cropping Images

When you're scanning for the Web, any cropping of the image that you do to select the area to be scanned serves two purposes. First, cropping can improve composition, an important part of making an image look better. Second, it makes the finished image file smaller. Therefore, whether you are sending it with e-mails or it is part of a web page, the image downloads faster. When cropping an image to improve composition, remember the purpose is to focus the attention of the viewer onto the subject. Photo composition is covered in greater detail in Chapter 11.

6

Attach a Photo to Your E-mail

You can use several different methods to attach a photo to an e-mail to send over the Internet. You can embed the photo in the e-mail so it appears as part of the e-mail, or you can attach the photo, in much the same way as you would attach any file.

The easiest way to send a photo or file to someone is to attach it. When you attach the photo to the e-mail, you won't see the photo—just an icon indicating an attached file, as shown next.

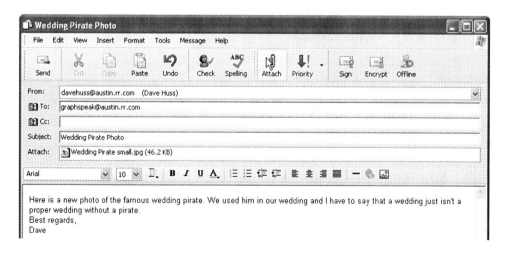

When the e-mail is received, how it actually appears depends upon the operating system and web browser being used. Generally, if the attached file is in JPEG format, the attached image will be displayed at the bottom of the e-mail like the one shown next.

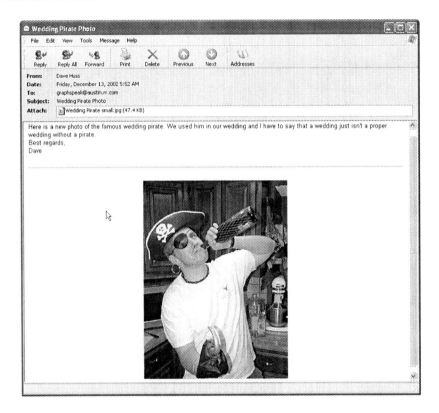

How to Attach Your Photo to an E-mail

Here is how to attach a photo to an e-mail using Outlook Express, but it works in a similar fashion with most e-mail programs:

1. Start a new e-mail by clicking the Send Mail button in the menu.

2. Select Insert | File, and the Insert File dialog box opens. From the dialog box, select the file of your photo and click the Insert button.

When looking for a photo, you may find it much easier to find the one you are looking for if you change the view to Thumbnails, as shown next (if your operating system supports it).

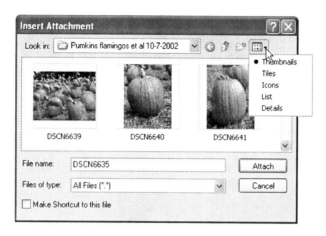

3. Add the usual e-mail stuff, like subject, address, and so on, and click the Send button.

Embed a Photo in Your E-mail

If your e-mail software supports HTML (a very popular Internet format), you have the option to embed photos in the e-mail. Figure 6-4 shows an example of an e-mail with embedded photos.

Inserting a photo into an e-mail isn't much more involved than attaching it. Here is how it is done:

1. Start a new e-mail by clicking the Create Mail button in the menu bar.

2. Verify that your e-mail is formatted as HTML. To do this in Outlook Express, click the Format button and check to see that "HTML" (some earlier versions of Outlook Express may say "Rich Text (HTML)") has a check mark beside it, as shown next.

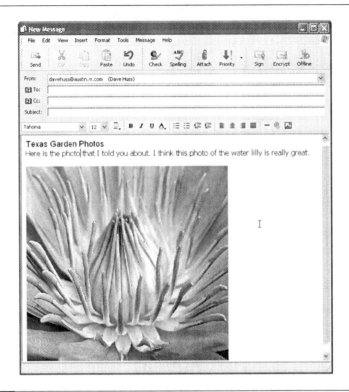

FIGURE 6-4 Embedding photos into an e-mail can produce very exciting e-mail.

3. Click the cursor at the place in the e-mail that you want to place the photo. In the toolbar, click the Insert Picture button, or choose Insert | Picture from the command menus to open the Picture dialog shown next.

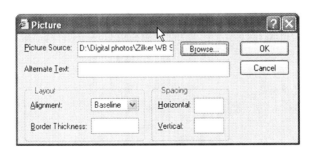

4. Click the Browse button, and then find and select the file. Once the file is selected, clicking the Open button returns you to the New Message window. Clicking OK inserts the photo at the insertion point.

5. By default the photo is placed at the insertion point. If it is too large (shame on you), the photo will appear at its native size, and scroll bars will display on the sides of the e-mail, as shown next.

6

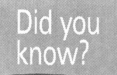

Not All E-mails Are Viewed Equally

Be aware of some considerations when embedding photos. First, not all operating systems or mail servers can properly read e-mail that is formatted as an HTML file. I used to send out a weekly newsletter with several photos embedded in it until I discovered that users of old Macintosh systems and most of my friends running mail software under Linux either couldn't see the embedded photos or in some cases couldn't even read the e-mail. There is no easy solution to this issue. My solution was to send a separate e-mail, which contained the original text, but the photos were sent as attached files to anyone who requested it.

6. You can resize a photo that is embedded in an e-mail by clicking the photo, causing control handles to appear at the corner (as shown next), and dragging any of the corners to resize the apparent size of the photo. I say "apparent" because the original image size doesn't actually change at all, only the displayed image.

 *To prevent distortion of an image, you should resize the picture using the corner handles, which maintain the picture's original proportions (aspect ratio).*

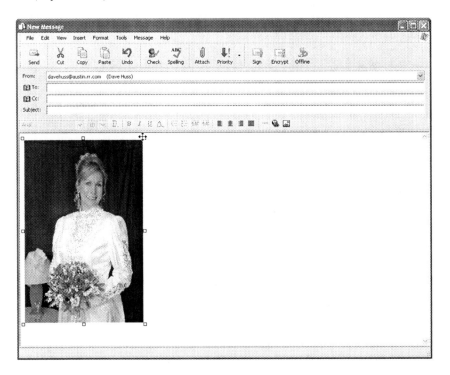

Getting a Photo out of an E-mail

Possibly the most-asked question I get concerning photos in e-mail involves receiving them. Typically, someone receives a great photo in an e-mail and wants to know how to save the photo apart from the e-mail. It is so easy—here's how:

1. Open the e-mail (don't just preview it in the mailbox).

2. Place the cursor on the photo, and click the right mouse button. A secondary pop-up menu like the one shown next appears. Choose Save Picture As.

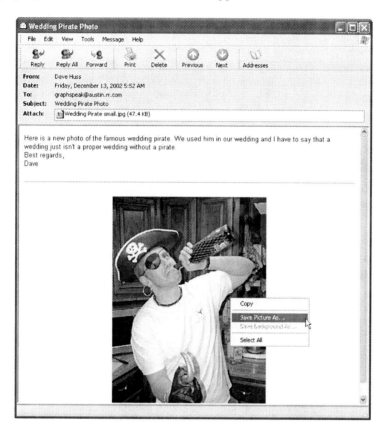

3. When the next dialog box appears, pick a location and save the file. The file format will be determined in part by the file format of the embedded photo. Sometimes you have the option to save a JPEG as a BMP, but most of the time you can only save the image in the format that it was when attached. You can always change the format later in a photo-editing program.

Scan for E-mail and Printing

If the photo in the e-mail was scanned at a low resolution to make it download quickly, it won't print very well unless you like really small photos. So how do you scan a photo small enough to send in an e-mail and still print? You have two alternatives. First, scan the image twice at two different resolutions, producing a print version and a web version. A better solution is to scan it at the resolution needed to print, and then open the file using a photo editor like Photoshop Elements, Paint Shop Pro, PhotoImpact, and so on. Next, resize it smaller, and use File | Save As to save a smaller JPEG copy of the image. I recommend putting some telltale word in the filename so that you can select the right file when embedding it into an e-mail. The method that works for me is adding the word "small" to the filename. For example, I had a large panorama image (over 30MB) named "Daybreak.TIF." When I resized it for my web page, I named it "Daybreak small.JPEG." Another solution resolves this issue automatically and is described in the next section.

Automated E-mail Photos

The creators of some photo-editing software (like Photoshop Elements 2) know how time-consuming resizing and attaching a photo to an e-mail can be. So, they provide an automatic feature that converts images to the correct size for attaching to an e-mail, and then launches your e-mail application with the e-mail attached! All you need to do is open the image in Photoshop Elements and click File | Attach to E-mail. If the image is too large (wider than 1200 pixels), a warning message like the one shown next will appear.

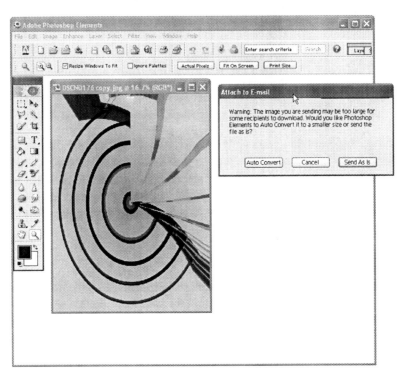

After you click the Auto Convert button, Elements makes a copy of the image, resizes the copy, and attaches it to an e-mail ready for you to send.

Sharing Photos Online

An alternative to sending photos to friends and others via e-mail is to post them on one of the many free web-based photo services. Most of these services are structured in a similar way in that they provide web-based storage and presentation for your scanned images that can be viewed by others. Figure 6-5 shows one of the albums I keep on the NikonNet service.

When these web-based photo services began, several of the pioneer sites folded after less than a year. Today most of the popular sites are owned by major organizations

6

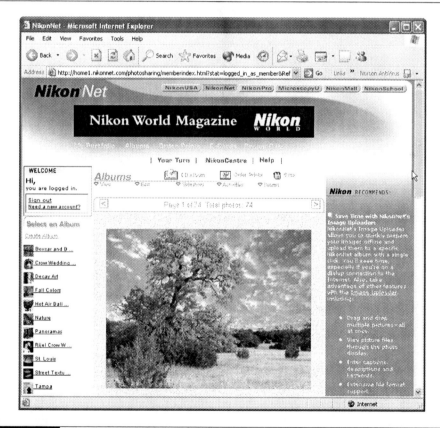

FIGURE 6-5   Web-based photo sites provide a free and easy way to share photos.

or camera companies. For example, Ofoto is owned by Kodak. Several major corporations, including the investment side of Adobe, own Shutterfly, shown next.

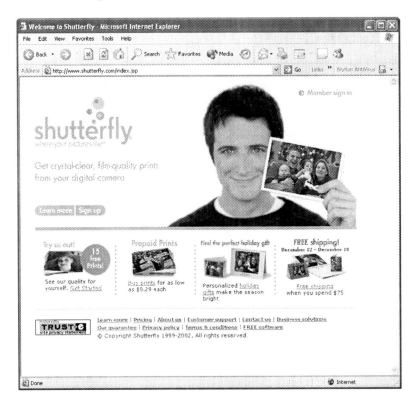

Examples of some of the more popular web-based services are

- Shutterfly (www.shutterfly.com)
- Webshots (www.webshots.com)
- Ofoto (www.ofoto.com)
- NikonNet (www.nikon.net)

Most of these services are free and only require that you register for the service. They usually offer a host of services. Once you've uploaded the pictures from your scanner, you can correct the red eye, fix the colors if they're a bit off, crop the picture to make sure your intended subject is the center of attention, and even attach fun creative borders to make it extra special. Then, with the click of your mouse, you can order prints and have them sent to you and your friends, or share your online albums with anyone you choose.

These web-based services usually offer an automated method for uploading the images from your computer to their site. Such services make their money by providing prints of the photos to viewers. For example, if you post a graduation photo of your daughter in an online album, the grandparents can view it online and order photographic prints, or have the image printed on a greeting card, coffee cup, T-shirt, or even a cookie. A few of the services that Ofoto offers are shown next.

Scanning for Web-Based Photo Services

This brings up an important issue regarding the scanning of images for these online photo services. You must decide in advance whether you expect the images you post to be printed or just viewed. If the images are only for viewing using an online photo album, then you want to make them low resolution (100 dpi or less, depending on the size of the original photo). If you want these photos to be printed, then you will need to scan the images at a size that will allow them to produce a quality print. Here is how to scan a photo that will be used for printing from a web-based photo service:

1. Prepare the scanner and image for scanning.

2. Set the destination or output setting to color photo/millions of colors. Do not use any of the Web or Internet settings.

3. If your scanner software asks for the output device, pick a color printer. This will scan the image at a resolution between 150 and 200 dpi.

4. Save the image as either a TIFF or JPEG file. I recommend saving it as a JPEG at a high-quality setting.

Scanning the photo at the higher resolution will produce a much larger file. This large file size will not prevent the photo from being viewed online, because all of these services have software that displays a smaller version of your photo file in their online albums.

Make the Right Choice—For You

We've looked at the many ways that you can scan, save, and send images that are destined for the World Wide Web. I sometimes am asked which technique or web-based service of the ones I've mentioned I use. The answer is I use them all. When I need to send several images to someone, I usually just attach them. When I want to send just one picture, like the one of my son, Jonathan, (yes, I have now exposed the secret identity of the wedding pirate), I will usually embed the photo. When I want to shoot a wedding, I will most often make an album and send an e-mail to the interested parties giving them the link to the web site. Now that we have covered this colorful topic, in the next chapter we will learn how to deal with the least colorful topic—optical character recognition (OCR).

Chapter 7

Scan Documents Using OCR Software

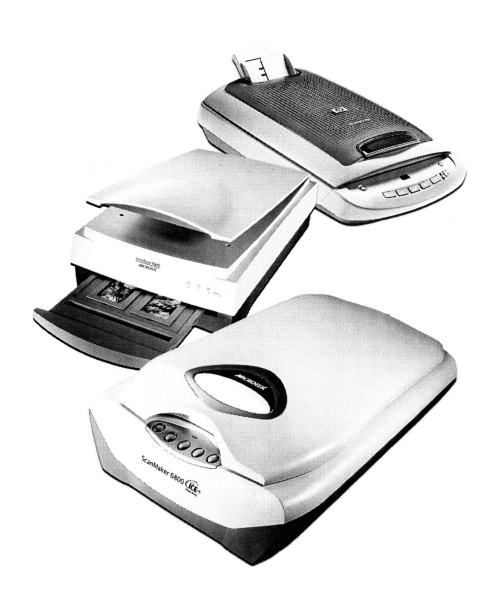

How to...

- Pick the best scanner for OCR
- Select the best OCR software
- Resolve OCR problems

The first time I saw OCR software for desktop PCs demonstrated was with an old operating system called DOS. Here's how it worked: After scanning in a document, the user told the computer the name of the typeface used (Times Roman, Helvetica, and so on) and the size of the type (in points). The computer would then work on the document for several minutes before producing a text file of the document. It all worked seamlessly in the demonstration, assuming the paper was laid in the scanner perfectly straight and there weren't any underlines, special characters, smudges, or handwritten annotations on the document being scanned. I was writing for a computer magazine at the time, and as I remember the results of the test we ran, by the time we finished checking the page for errors and correcting them, it

Why Your Scanned Text Cannot Be Edited

A popular misconception about using scanners with printed text usually goes like this. A user scans in a document and tries to load it directly into a word processor, only to discover it won't work. If this has ever happened to you, here's why it didn't work. When a sheet of printed paper is scanned, the result is a "picture" of the printed page, not the actual text. While the picture of the text can be read by a human viewer, the word processor doesn't see it as anything except a bitmap file, just the same as if it were a graphic picture. Many scanners sold today have a button on the front with an icon indicating that the scanner performs OCR when the button is pressed. In fact, pushing the button starts an OCR program that was installed on your computer (along with a lot of other software) when the scanner software was originally installed. It is that software that tells the scanner to scan the document and perform the conversion of the scanned image into text.

would have been faster to type the document (assuming we could type 40 words per minute (WPM)). The accuracy of these early OCR programs was so poor it is surprising how far they have come in the last 15 years.

How OCR Is Accomplished

OCR programs organize the patterns of pixels that come from the scanner into characters using a variety of techniques to determine what the characters are. While that sounds easy, it is a very complex task. As a human viewing this document, you see the characters on this page as symbols. We have memorized the shape of the characters and recognize them when we view them. An OCR program doesn't see the characters like we do; instead it must analyze thousands of pixels that are either black or white and determine what pixels belong together. The earliest OCR program (1959) could read just one font at one size and was used for processing preprinted mortgage loan applications in the banking industry. Later OCR programs were created that could read ten or more fonts using *template matching,* in which an image was compared with a library of bitmap images. Accuracy was good as long as the fonts in the library matched those being read. Today's programs can read just about everything we can scan.

When OCR Does and Doesn't Make Good Sense

OCR work can be generally grouped into three categories:

- Commercial
- Heavy office usage
- Occasional office usage

A Glimpse at Commercial OCR

The work done by large OCR shops is impressive. They use scanners that are specifically designed for OCR work. Most of these scanners can scan up to 100 pages per minute and cost upwards of $40,000. The most common job performed by these shops is the conversion of paper documents (like all of those charge card slips that you sign) into electronic documents for archival storage. Another common task is the conversion of printed documents (like old books) into electronic format.

Heavy/Occasional Office Usage

I define "heavy" office usage as an environment where OCR-related work is done every day and where it is an integral part of the daily workflow. An example of a heavy-use office environment is a legal office that must scan and convert hundreds of typed reports during the discovery phase of an investigation. OCR use enables them to search the documents for specific words or phrases in less than a minute, rather than weeks. The occasional-use office is one in which when someone wants to perform OCR, they have to ask someone how it is done or knock the dust off the OCR software users manual before they can scan a document.

What's the Best Scanner for OCR?

Almost any scanner sold today can be used to perform OCR, although not all scanners do OCR well. The type of scanner required depends on whether your work environment need for OCR is heavy or occasional. If you expect to be doing a lot of OCR work, you must make sure that your scanner has an automatic document feeder (ADF) like the one shown in Figure 7-1.

 *If you have had poor experience with older scanner ADFs made in the early 1990s, they have since vastly improved.*

A good rule of thumb for selecting a dedicated (or heavy use) OCR scanner is that if it comes with an ADF, it will work fine. This is a good rule, but there are

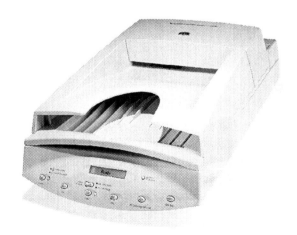

FIGURE 7-1   The automatic document feeder is essential for large amounts of OCR.

other things to consider when choosing between several scanners that come equipped with an ADF:

- Is the scanner supported by your OCR software?

- How high is the scanner's resolution?

- What is the size of the scanning area?

- How fast is your scanner?

Is Your Scanner Supported?

This question is most important if you are considering the purchase of a new scanner for use with a particular software program. While all scanners may seem alike, some offer features that the OCR software can control to produce more accurate results for OCR work. For this reason, you should go to the web site for your OCR software (in almost all cases it will be www.scansoft.com), and see if your scanner is on the list, like the one shown next, of the scanners that each product supports.

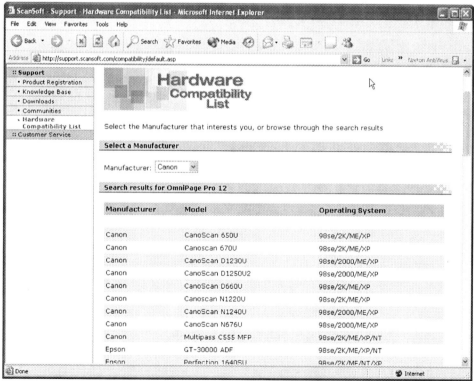

If you are considering the use of an existing scanner with the OCR software, you should be aware that there are many older scanners available with ADFs that may not be a good choice when working with current OCR software—even if they are supported. If your existing ADF scanner is supported, you still may want to consider replacing it, because ADF units have improved tremendously in just the past five years. The newer units experience fewer jams and misalignments than the older ones.

How High Is Your Scanner Resolution?

Though today's scanners are advertising incredibly high resolutions, documents that will be converted to text will be scanned at 300 dpi or 400 dpi. Most OCR programs will accept either. The higher the resolution of your scan, the longer it takes to scan the page. On the other hand, when you're scanning very small fonts, the higher-resolution scan will allow the OCR software to do a better job recognizing the characters in the text. For example, at 300 dpi, your scanning will be done faster, but at 400 dpi, you may get better results, especially on small type.

Check the Scanning Area Size

A further consideration when buying a scanner is the maximum size image a particular unit can scan. Among flatbed scanners, particular units are divided between those that can scan only a letter-size (8.5×11") page and those that can

When High Resolution Isn't That High

When looking at the resolution stated by the scanner manufacturer, you should be aware that an increasing number of scanners are using lenses to increase the resolution available in one part of the scanning bed, by concentrating the light reflected off the image. This accommodates the scanning of slides and negatives that require scanning at high resolution. Though the scanner can scan at the higher resolution, it can be misleading if the high-resolution area only covers a small part of the overall scanning area. Be on the lookout for scanners that advertise dual resolutions, and be aware that the highest resolution will probably only be available for small images and therefore not available for OCR scanning.

handle a full legal-size (8.5×14") scan. Letter-size scanners are sometimes referred to as "A4-sized," in reference to the European paper-sizing system. In choosing a scanner, consider if it is necessary to have a full legal-sized scanning bed (because these scanners tend to be more expensive). Few users need this capability, but for realtors, lawyers, and others who work with these larger documents, the larger scanning area is essential.

How Fast Is Your Scanner?

The last thing to check when you are shopping for a scanner is the unit's speed. The importance of the scanner's speed depends on how many times you intend to use it. Those scanning once or twice a day will certainly be less bothered by a slow scanner than those who are constantly performing OCR.

Unfortunately, determining scanning speed isn't easy, because there is no single standard for evaluating the time it takes to complete a scanning operation. Manufacturers frequently specify the raw speed of their scanner motors (this number is usually expressed in milliseconds per line, or ms/ln), but that speed rarely correlates with real-world performance. Other considerations, including the speed of the scanner's driver software, the overall power and memory capacity of your computer connected to the scanner, and the type of connection (USB 1.1, USB 2.0, or IEEE 1394) between it and the computer, all affect the overall performance.

The only real way to evaluate a scanner's speed would be to try a few sample scans, which in the average computer superstore is impossible because they are never hooked up. The best alternative is to find a magazine's web site and to search for reviews on the scanner or scanners that you are considering. These reviews usually provide fairly useful comparisons. When using these comparisons, though, be sure to take into account that if the review focuses on a different aspect of scanning, like photo scanning, the results may have no impact on the way you will be using the scanner.

What Can OCR Software Do?

While the original OCR applications were limited to converting printed text to text that could be edited on a computer, the applications that are available today can do much, much more. Here is a partial list of what can be done using your scanner and one of these OCR-based applications:

- Convert a printed spreadsheet into a worksheet that can be read by Excel or any of the other spreadsheet programs.

7

- Scan in a complete document containing columns and tables and convert it into a word processing document with the tables in the document functioning as tables and the columns intact.

- Extract graphics from a document. Documents containing images (photos, signatures, handwritten notation) can save these images as separate graphic images.

- Scan a form and convert it into an electronic version of the same form.

- Manage paper documents by scanning in a document (receipt, newspaper article, warranty, and so on), have the OCR portion of the program convert the text portion, and then store a copy of the image. This same program can later locate the document for you based on a word search and print you a copy.

Which OCR Software Is Best?

First of all, the OCR software that came with your scanner is almost always a limited version of a more robust version or more likely is an older version of the software. If you are only going to do OCR work occasionally, then you should try to use the software that came with your scanner. Be aware, however, that the ability of the free OCR software may be so restricted that it may not work well enough for even occasional use.

There are several different OCR software applications in today's market, and here is my favorite part—most are offered by the same company. See the sidebar "Why Are There So Many Names but Only One Company?" When deciding which OCR application to purchase, you must first consider your office needs. Not all of the OCR applications can read a multicolumn document and re-create the columns in the final document. If you will be scanning a lot of financial information in the form of spreadsheets and tables, make sure that the OCR program you choose can convert the printed information into actual spreadsheets and tables.

Prepare to Convert a Document Using OCR

While the exact procedure for scanning and converting a document depends on the OCR software you are using, some preparatory steps are common to all of the programs. OCR programs have the same requirements as any ordinary copy work. In Chapter 3, we covered the importance of properly positioning the original on

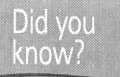

Why Are There So Many Names But Only One Company?

When OCR software began to appear on Windows systems, two major companies advertised heavily how much better their product was than their competitor. So, it came as a surprise when the two companies merged. After many successive mergers and acquisitions, today that company is called ScanSoft. While there are other OCR software companies, ScanSoft's applications dominate the market. When you go to their web page (www.scansoft.com), you will find that they offer several OCR applications each under its original name. OmniPage Pro is their industrial-strength product, TextBridge is their mid-range OCR package, and Pagis is a combination package of several different scanning OCR-type products.

the scanner glass. For OCR work, the need for an image to be as straight as possible is even more critical because of the way the program reads the scanned image. If the document in the scanner is crooked, the OCR program has greater difficulty determining and converting the text or other images. This results in more errors in the final text or more time spent in the proofreading portion of the OCR process. If you are placing each sheet in the scanner manually, you need to make sure the sheet lines up with the scanner edge (assuming that it is letter or legal size). This can really become a problem with photocopies where the original wasn't laid straight on the copy glass. If it only involves a few sheets of paper, here is a solution that has always worked for me:

1. Place the document face down on a light table, a glass table, or on a window. Do whatever it takes to get enough light coming through the paper so that you can see what is printed on the side that is to be scanned.

2. Take the plastic triangle and with a pencil lightly draw a line on the back of the paper that is parallel with a line of text on the printed side.

3. Place the document face down on the scanner glass and use the same plastic triangle to position the paper on the glass so the line you just drew is perpendicular to the edge of the scanner glass.

If you are using an ADF, here are some things you can do to make sure that it feeds the document in straight.

The Proper Care and Feeding of ADFs

The ADF on most of the scanners I have worked with will do a good job of moving and positioning the document on the scanner if you pay attention to the following rules:

- Don't exceed the maximum number of pages allowed in the ADF input tray. Load no more than the maximum rated number of pages, and remove pages from the output bin if they are stacking up.

- Ensure the documents loaded in the input tray meet the specifications for the ADF. Most ADFs will jam if the paper being scanned is too thick, and they will pass multiple sheets at a time if they are too thin. If your media fits either of these categories, you will have to place your documents on the scanner glass manually.

- If the pages look like they are skewing as they feed into the ADF, check the resulting scanned images in the software to ensure they are not skewed. If the results show a skewed image, the item may be incorrectly placed in the input tray. Straighten the item and adjust the paper guides to center the stack.

- A common problem is papers that have foreign objects on them. Make sure you have removed anything such as staples and stuck-on notes from the item.

- Ensure the document is square or rectangular and in good condition (not fragile or worn). It should be free from tears, perforations, punch holes, wet glue, correction fluid, or ink. Don't even try to feed multipart forms with carbon pages through an ADF. Transparencies and light onionskin pages also shouldn't be used because they will not feed correctly.

- Make sure the paper is the correct size. Most ADFs can handle items as small as 3.5×5", but check the documentation of your scanner to make sure. If the item being scanned is smaller than the dimensions listed, you must place it manually on the glass to scan.

- Verify that the paper size selected in the software is correct. The default paper size is set to Letter. If using media other than Letter size, adjust the paper size setting in your ADF Scan dialog box of your scanning software.

Things that Confuse OCR Software

Humans are incredible creatures; we can read a document like the one shown in Figure 7-2 without much problem. To an OCR program it is a nightmare. The following are the most common things that trip up many OCR programs:

- **Smeared or colored text** The text that is smeared in Figure 7-2 isn't hard for a human to read, but the light smearing of the characters makes it very difficult for the computer to determine what characters are on the page.

- **Underlined text** The underlined text in Figure 7-2 is sloppy handwritten underlining, but even if the underlining is part of the machine text, it can still confuse OCR programs, especially if the text is very small (6–8 points).

7

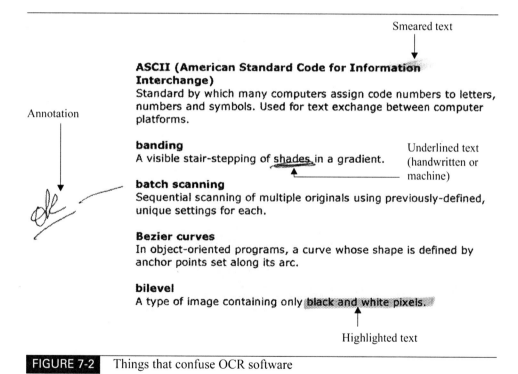

FIGURE 7-2 Things that confuse OCR software

■ **Annotations**   When we see the "OK" written in the example, we know what it is. The OCR program will think it is a graphic or will create some imaginative interpretation of what text it thinks it is.

■ **Highlighted text**   Depending on the color, this can drive an OCR program wild.

■ **Fancy display fonts**   Some of the really exotic fonts can confuse the best programs.

■ **Bleed through**   If the printing on the other side of the paper can be seen, the OCR program may be fooled and think that the other side's text is supposed to be converted.

■ **Sloppy copies or faxes**   Did you ever get a document that was a copy of a copy of a copy? If the text is mushy and difficult for you to read, then you can rest assured that the OCR program will have problems as well.

■ **Multicolumned original**   When a multicolumn document is converted by an OCR application that doesn't support this feature, the first line in column A and the first line in column B become one sentence (which sometimes makes really funny reading material). Fear not, most of today's OCR applications support multicolumn conversion; in some cases, you just need to turn it on.

How to Perform OCR on Colored Paper

A real OCR challenge is text that is printed on colored paper, especially dark colored paper. There is a manual (no ADF) solution:

1. Perform a preview scan.

2. Set the Color mode to Line Art at a resolution of 300 dpi.

3. Manually adjust the Threshold setting until the background color disappears from the preview window.

4. Scan and save the image.

5. Open it with the OCR software and process it.

6. Make a mental note not to accept any documents printed on colored paper ever again.

Prevent Bleed Through

If the printing on the back of the document you are scanning is visible, you can easily prevent it. Place a sheet of black construction paper behind the page you are scanning. The dark color will reduce the reflection of the light through the page against the white underside of the copy lid and reduce or prevent the bleed through.

Scan for OCR

7

All of the current OCR programs actually control the scanning process, so in most cases it is no longer necessary to scan the document, save it, and then open it with the OCR program (unless it was on colored paper). The procedure differs between the different OCR programs, but in general the steps are as follows:

1. The program scans in the document(s).

2. After each page is scanned, the software performs OCR on it.

3. Each time the software encounters a word it suspects is incorrect, it will show you the actual scanned character or word in question, and ask you to either correct it or accept it. It remembers the correction so that the next time the same word, symbol, or character is encountered, it will apply the same correction as you instructed before.

4. Once all the pages have been scanned and converted, the program will ask in what application format to save the finished work. Most OCR programs will also offer the option to save the original OCR processed file, which can be opened later and reprocessed or output in a format for a different application.

Now that we have covered the basic principles of OCR, in the next chapter, we will learn how to use both the OCR applications and other scanner features in the office workplace.

Chapter 8

Use Your Scanner for a Variety of Workplace Tasks

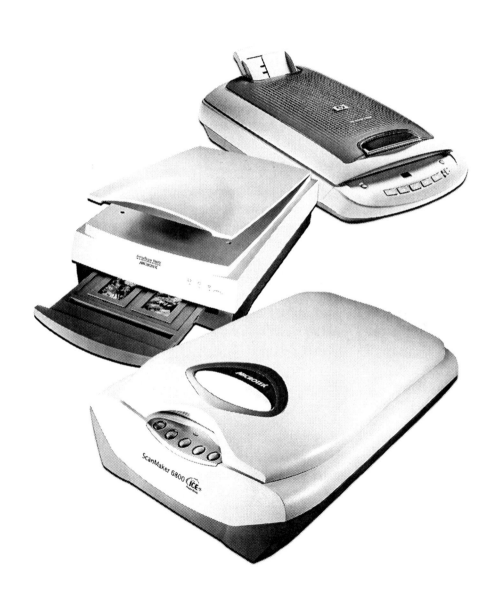

How to...

■ Scan business cards

■ Choose the best scanner for electronic communication

■ Use your scanner to send a fax

■ Use the scanner to manage office paperwork

Most people think of scanners in a very limited capacity when it comes to general office work. Ask what a scanner in an office is used for, and the usual answer will be to scan pictures. In the previous chapter, we learned that scanners can be used for many of the typical functions of a small office/home office (SOHO). In this chapter, we will explore additional capabilities of scanners in the workplace. We'll begin with the reading and conversion of business cards into electronic address books.

Scan Business Cards

Did you know that business cards have been around for more than 300 years? In the days of Queen Victoria, they were referred to as "calling cards." Later, they became known as "trade cards." Around the turn of the century, Albert Einstein and Henry Ford were among the first to use what we now call business cards. Without a scanner, you must manually enter the information from a business card into software specifically designed to manage such information. Often this software is called either a *personal information manager (PIM)* or a *contact manager.* One application with PIM capability with which you may be familiar is the Outlook program in Microsoft Windows. Other popular applications include the following:

■ Act

■ Goldmine

■ Lotus Notes

Once the information is in the application, it becomes a simple matter to use it or transfer it to your *personal data assistant (PDA).* Because the business card scanning software depends on the processing power of a desktop or laptop to perform the OCR on the business card, you cannot yet attach the card scanner directly to a PDA or PIM. They simply do not have the horsepower to do the job.

If you plan on using the business card scanner on the road, you may want to consider getting one of the newer USB-powered scanners that do not require an AC adapter.

The first time I saw a card scanner at the Comdex computer trade show many years ago, it worked well only as long as the business cards had crisp dark type on a white background and no graphics. But when you fed it a card with a colored background, elaborate graphics, or an artistic typeface, it choked. The result was that more time was spent correcting the scanner's mistakes than you would have spent typing the information. These scanners have come a long way since then. Today, a card scanner can be expected to correctly scan and identify all of the data on the card with little to no operator intervention. The newest versions of these scanners can even preserve the original card, like the one shown next, for later viewing; the software also includes the ability to save cards in separate categories (for example, business and personal). When it comes to business card scanners and software, the CardScan series of scanners and software by Corex (www.cardscan.com) owns a majority of this unique market.

Two Ways to Scan Business Cards

You can scan data from business cards into your application in two ways. You must either use a dedicated card scanner or use business card scanning software (usually sold by the same company that sells the card scanners) with your flatbed scanner to scan business cards into your computer. Dedicated card scanners are the best method to scan business cards into your application if you are scanning many cards. If you accumulate a lot of cards over the course of your business, then a dedicated business card scanner like the CardScan 600c, shown in Figure 8-1, is a good investment.

Though these scanners will fit into the palm of your hand, they typically can cost several times more than a consumer flatbed scanner. One major advantage to using a dedicated business card scanner over using business card scanning software with your flatbed scanner involves processing speed. Since business cards are too small to be used with scanner automatic document feeders (ADFs), each business card must be positioned by hand, scanned, and removed from a flatbed scanner, which may actually take more time than an experienced typist needs to enter the data by keyboard. This is especially true if the typical business card you get is a graphic work of art. As both a graphic artist and a photographer, I receive many business cards that range from stunning to difficult to read and with which even the best card scanning program will need some help.

FIGURE 8-1   A business card scanner provides a way to rapidly input business data into your computer.

How a Scanner Reads a Business Card

Since business cards have no standards, it can be very difficult for a computer to read them. A good business card scanning application mimics the way we read the same cards. When viewing cards, we recognize proper names like "Tom" or "Julia" as individual names, whereas a phrase that ends with "Inc.," "Corp.," or "LLC" suggests a company name. Similarly, an "@" sign designates an e-mail address. Business card scanning programs follow a similar logic, using internal dictionaries of thousands of words and symbols in many languages to sort out what parts of the card fall into what category. Although the principles are simple, each business card may present unique challenges. Some have fancy fonts and graphics that cover a large portion of the card, and some have names that while common to their own culture, present a real challenge to a program attempting to determine if text is a name or a street address. Examples of such are the famous Indian film director Adoor Gopalakrishnan or the noted Polish cardiologist Dr. Leszek Ceremuzynski.

If the foreign name doesn't gag the spelling checker, some foreign-language character sets still can confuse some OCR applications, although most full-featured ones have little to no difficulty with language sets that only differ from English by a few unusual characters and accent marks.

8

Scanning Other Small Documents

In addition to being able to scan business cards, dedicated business card scanners can be used to scan driver's licenses, health insurance cards, and other forms of ID cards. The makers of the business card scanners sell software development tools that allow programmers to develop software for a wide variety of specialty applications. The only real limits to the possibilities have to do with the physical size of the original being scanned—most business card scanners handle a size little larger than a standard business card and up to as large as 4×6 inches.

How to Scan a Business Card to Capture Logos or Other Art

Sometimes you will need to scan a business card to capture a logo or some other art that is on the card. If the card is in good shape, here is how to scan it:

1. Position the card on the scanner glass so that it is properly aligned as discussed in Chapter 3.

2. Do a preview scan of the card. Select the area of the art on the card, and zoom in on it as shown next:

3. Depending on the final size of the scanned art that is required, change the scaling of the image to the required size. I recommend increasing the size to at least 200%.

4. If the business card being scanned is black and white, scan it in as grayscale; if the card has color, scan it in as a color photo. If you are scanning a photo from a business, you must be pretty desperate for a photo, and you should ensure that de-screening is selected. Be aware that some scanning applications will display an error message if you attempt to apply de-screening to a very small image and enlarge it several hundred percent.

5. Scan the image and do any necessary cleanup with a photo-editing application like Paint Shop Pro or Photoshop Elements.

 *Art on business cards is not meant for further reproduction and has limited quality when reproduced. So no matter how good your scanner is or how much effort you put into it, you are limited as to how large you can make images captured from a business card.*

Scan for Electronic Communication

Not so long ago, every successful business had a dedicated fax machine for sending and receiving facsimiles of documents. (Did you know that "fax" stands for "facsimile transmission"?) With the increasing popularity of e-mail for business communication, fax machines are no longer the integral part of the office communication equipment that they once were. For this reason, many SOHO offices have chosen not to spend money for a dedicated fax machine that seldom sees use and have chosen rather to either buy a multifunction scanner/printer/fax machine or to use their scanner as a fax machine.

How to Choose the Best Scanner for Electronic Communication

When it comes time to select the best equipment to use for sending faxes, you can choose from two categories of equipment. Most scanner companies offer a multipurpose device that can work as a scanner, copier, printer, and a fax machine like the one shown next.

8

The other category of equipment for sending a fax is to use your flatbed scanner with either the fax software that may have shipped with it or with any of the fax applications that are available either online or from retailers.

The All-in-One Solution

The all-in-one solution equipment is a good choice if you do not require a high-resolution scanner or a high-volume printer. In the past, I wasn't fond of this type of equipment because none of the features was very good at what it did. For example, the scanner was only a fair scanner, and in the earlier units, the scanner was actually the same scanner used to copy and send faxes, which speaks volumes about the quality. The other disadvantage was (and still is) if the unit fails and must be repaired, you lose the availability of all of the equipment the unit contains.

Today, the multipurpose units can be connected to the computer, and they will act as a printer and a scanner. The scanner part of the unit can be used to produce good scans if the unit has a flatbed-style scanner and not a sheet-fed scanner. Don't confuse a unit with an ADF with a sheet-fed scanner. If your office has a limited budget and needs the ability to send and receive faxes, one of the multipurpose units should meet your needs.

Setting up these units does not require a computer; they only require AC power and access to a phone line to work. Sending a fax from one of these units is very similar to sending one from a fax machine.

Send a Fax from Your Scanner

Setting up and sending a fax from your flatbed scanner is a little more involved. There are two different ways to send a fax using your flatbed scanner. You can use the fax software that came with your scanner, or you can use a fax service.

The advantage of using the fax software that came with your scanner is cost. Other than any phone call costs, it doesn't cost you anything to send a fax. The disadvantage is the lack of a dedicated fax phone number (if you are using a regular voice line to send faxes) for receiving faxes. But if you are only sending faxes occasionally, this is an excellent way to send a fax. To send faxes this way, you must have the following:

- Computer with a fax modem installed

- Fax software installed on the computer

- Access to a phone line (doesn't have to be dedicated)

If your scanner provides a fax feature (and some do), the fax software would have been installed on your computer when the rest of the scanner software was installed. Typically, the fax software icon appears as a printer. While each scanner and its software has its own way to generate a fax, the procedure is as follows:

1. Place the copy to be sent on the scanner glass and replace the lid.

2. Press the Fax button (if available) on the front of the scanner. If there isn't a dedicated fax button, choose the Scan button.

3. When the pre view scan is finished, select the area you want to fax, as shown next.

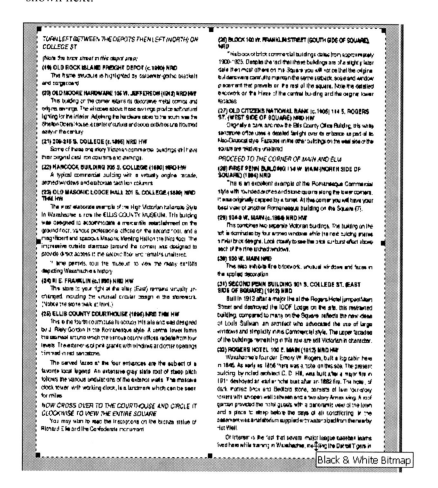

8

4. Choose the color mode. This can be either grayscale or black-and-white bitmap. If the document is printed on colored paper, you should consider using black-and-white bitmap. Whatever you choose, don't choose any color settings.

5. Select the Print button, choosing the fax printer as the destination. This action opens another dialog box that allows you to enter the phone number of the receiving fax machine.

Send a Photo by Fax

Sending a photo via a fax machine is the quickest way I know of to make a good photo look horrible. Traditionally, sending a photo via fax involves making a photocopy of the original and then sending the copy through a fax machine. This usually results in a muddy, difficult to decipher image at the other end. A much better way is to install an inexpensive fax modem in your personal computer, then use your scanner as the input device. Enhance your image with a photo editor like Photoshop Elements or Paint Shop Pro before you send it, and then apply a diffusion dither (at 100 or 150 dpi) found in most photo editors (under "filters") before you send the image. The resulting fax will be much more legible for the recipient.

Fax by the Buttons

While the easiest way to send a document is by attaching it to an e-mail, sometimes you need to send a document to an actual fax machine. When you fax a document using the buttons on your flatbed scanner, some scanners scan the document using default settings optimized for faxing. If you have a fax program that came with the scanner, the scanned image then automatically appears in a new fax message, which you then address and send. Do not make changes to the scanned image. When you fax using the scanner buttons, the scanner scans the item using default settings optimized for faxing. If your fax program is not supported, select "Fax" anyway. The computer scans the item using the optimal settings and prompts you to save the scanned image as a file. Open your fax program and attach the file to a message as you normally do.

Fax Using a Fax Service

If you need to be able to send and receive faxes on a regular basis, it is still possible to use your flatbed scanner to send them by using a fax service. You'll find several advantages to using a fax service over the method described in the preceding section. First, you don't need a dedicated phone line. This can be very handy in situations where the Internet access is via a cable modem and the phone connections go through a private branch exchange (PBX). For a monthly fee, the major fax services offer a dedicated local number or a toll-free number for receiving your faxes. They also offer the ability to receive faxes directly on your computer via e-mail rather than the crude printouts that we have come to associate with fax copies. Faxing through a nationwide service also has the benefit of sending a single fax to hundreds of recipients across the nation or around the world.

Send a Fax Using a Fax Service

Sending a fax via a fax service is similar to using a fax modem (with a few exceptions), which is shown next using eFax Messenger Plus:

1. Place the copy to be sent on the scanner glass and replace the lid.

2. Select Start | Programs, choose your fax service application, and then click Scan Document.

3. Choose the desired option from the Scan tab. When the Scanner Selection window pops up, select the scanner you want to use and click OK.

4. When the preview scan is finished, select the area you want to fax. With most fax services, it isn't necessary to be concerned about the color mode (grayscale, color, black-and-white, and so on) because the fax service processes the document before sending it to a fax machine.

5. There should be a dedicated button in the menu bar for the fax service. Clicking the Scan button opens another dialog box that allows you to enter the fax phone number and other information about the document you want to send. The next example shows the fax service that I use, eFax.com.

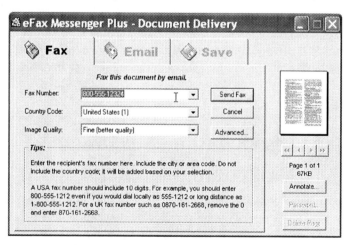

One last advantage of using electronic faxes over the traditional faxes is that it is possible to fax a document to someone without ever printing it. Whether you are using fax software with a fax modem or a fax service, you can print a document directly from an application like Microsoft Word or Excel to a virtual fax printer and have it faxed directly to the recipient's fax machine. Here is how it is done:

1. Create the document you want to fax—don't forget a cover sheet since it will be eventually sent to a real fax machine.

2. Print the document to the printer that is designated as the fax printer. It isn't a real printer but a virtual printer that serves as the portal to the fax software.

3. When the next dialog box opens, you will be prompted for a phone number of the receiving fax machine(s) and other details, like what fax mode (normal, fine, detail).

 *When printing documents as faxed documents, remember that the quality of the receiving fax machine is usually minimal, so you should avoid photographs or areas of spreadsheets that have color shading, which could appear as black squares on the receiving fax machine.*

Send an Image as an E-mail Attachment

If you installed the software that came with your scanner, attaching an image to an e-mail is pretty simple. Here is how it is accomplished:

1. Click the e-mail button on the front of the scanner. You might receive a message box like the one shown next when you click the button. This is a message from the operating system asking you what action to take anytime that button is pressed. In the example shown, I have selected the software that is associated with the scanner that I am using. If you are not sure which one

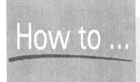 ## Attach a Signature to an Electronic Document

Using a fax to send notes and letters directly to the recipient (from within the word processing applications) saves time and paper, but it usually means your correspondence arrives without your signature. You can solve that problem by scanning in your signature, saving it as a TIFF or JPEG file, and then dropping it into your electronic documents right where it belongs. It is a great way to add a personal touch to your computer communications.

to use, don't check the Always Use This Program For This Action
check box.

2. When the image appears in the preview window of the HP scanning
software, correct the orientation (from portrait to landscape) if necessary.

3. Since we want to attach the photo to an e-mail, I choose the e-mail icon on
the right side of the dialog box, which opens another dialog box as shown
next, and choose the small (for viewing) option.

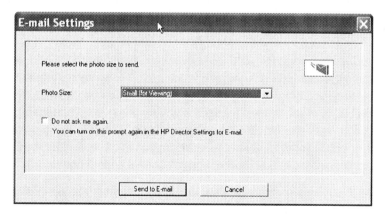

4. Clicking Send To E-mail opens a new e-mail in your default e-mail
application, and after resizing the photo, it attaches the file to the e-mail.
All that is required is for you to address it.

The first time that you automatically attach a scanned image to an e-mail, you
may discover that the scanner program thinks that your default e-mail program is
Outlook rather than the more commonly used Outlook Express. This results in

your address book or your contact list being empty. Don't panic; just change the default mail settings in your scanning program so that it launches Outlook Express rather than Outlook when attaching an image to an e-mail.

 *If you are scanning printed material (like a photo in a magazine), make sure that you select the de-screen option to prevent moiré patterns on the scanned image.*

Another issue you may discover is that most scanner programs attach images to e-mail rather than embedding them in an HTML format e-mail. If you are sending this e-mail to a variety of recipients, attachment is a better choice since some browsers cannot accept HTML documents. The good news is that if you are sending the e-mail to another Windows user, the JPEG file will display automatically when it is opened.

Convert Printed Pages to Text (OCR)

This topic was covered in the previous chapter, but a few items about OCR in the office workplace deserve repeating. The most important issue is using some advance planning before starting an OCR project. Here are some issues to consider when converting documents to text using OCR:

- *How big is the project?* If you are converting a page or less, it might take you less time to type the document than to scan it, apply OCR, and proof the results.

- *Does the document contain foreign words or discipline-specific terms?* One of the ways that OCR programs do their magic is by converting the scanned characters and then doing a spelling check. If the document contains many technical, medical, or legal terms, it will slow down the proofreading portion of the OCR work the first few times that you do it. Good OCR programs offer the ability to build up a dictionary of words and terms. Use this feature if you are going to continue to use OCR to convert similar printed documents.

- *How clean is the original document?* If the original you are converting contains a lot of handwritten annotation, smears, or highlighting, it will slow down the proofreading portion of the OCR scanning considerably. If the document is too badly marked up, consider typing it in manually.

- *Is the original a book or bound pamphlet?* Like it or not, the only effective way to use OCR with these type of documents is to dismantle them and scan them one page at a time. If you attempt to scan a book without taking it apart, the pages will bend at the spine, the text will be distorted, and the OCR program will not be able to recognize the parts near the spine.

■ *Is the original available in PDF format?* Some OCR programs offer the ability to read a PDF file and convert it to another editable document format like Microsoft Word. This can be a real timesaver. Not long ago, the only way to convert a PDF file into a different format was to print the PDF, scan it, and then use OCR to make it into an editable document.

Convert Printed Forms to Electronic Ones

Paper forms are a pain. For years, companies have been trying to make a program that will allow you to scan in the original form and turn it into an electronic one. While working on this book, I used a program named OmniForm from ScanSoft that provides a quick way to convert paper forms to a digital one that can be filled in onscreen. The resulting data can be managed without programming experience—which is good since I just discovered that C++ is a programming language and not a vitamin supplement.

Even in a small office, replacing your existing printed fill-in-the-squares forms with electronic ones reduces errors, increases productivity, and is just an overall good idea. This program also allowed me to quickly create a few forms for use around my office. Industry studies show that on average, electronic forms can save over $100 in per-form transaction (the cost of manual data entry of handwritten forms) compared with paper forms. While larger organizations may have the staff and budget to create electronic forms, smaller organizations often feel stuck with the old paper forms. I was able to convert one of my forms in a matter of a few minutes and used one of their pre-made forms to create a cool one for keeping track of my mileage when traveling on photo shoots.

Form data gathered by an electronic form can be collected in a database that is automatically created for each form, which provides for easy data analysis. Data can be exported to ODBC-compliant databases such as MS Access and Oracle. Open Database Connectivity (ODBC) is a widely accepted application programming interface (API) for database access.

Use Your Scanner as a Copier

With the availability of inexpensive color copiers, the need to use your scanner and printer as a copier isn't as popular as it was a few years ago. Still, you may need to make color copies now and again, and if you don't have a dedicated office copier, you can use your scanner to make them. The advantage of using a scanner as a copier is its ability to make high-quality color copies. You can also make standard copy adjustments, such as reducing or enlarging, or lightening or darkening. You can also choose a printer other than the default printer. The disadvantage is that the number of copies that can be made is limited by the output speed of the printer you are using, and the cost per copy is more expensive than with a standard photocopier.

To use your scanner as a copier, do the following:

1. Press the Copy button on the scanner, which will launch a copy program that was installed along with your scanner software.

2. When the copy dialog box opens (like the one shown next), change the settings as appropriate. Select the desired printer (if you are not using the default printer). Select the type of original, and adjust the number of copies.

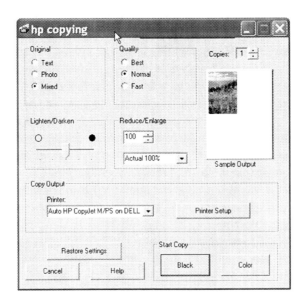

3. Choose the type of output (color or black-and-white) in the Start Copy box.

While the exact procedures vary with different types of scanners and software, almost all of the copy utilities operate the same way. The copy utility for a Canon scanner is shown next.

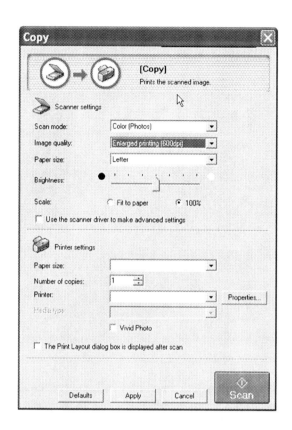

Scanners—the Ultimate File Cabinet

Back in the 1970s, everyone began talking about the paperless office of the future. If you work in an office, you know that there is nothing paperless about it. A lot more paper seems to be flying around today than I remember from 30 years ago. You can use your scanner and a program named PaperPort (shown next) to manage this paper tsunami. PaperPort enables you to scan, store, organize, retrieve, and use paper documents on your computer along with all of your existing PC documents. Managing documents is easy with this program. Thumbnails are created for each popular document type, and then the documents are "stacked" in the correct piles, making it much easier to locate your files.

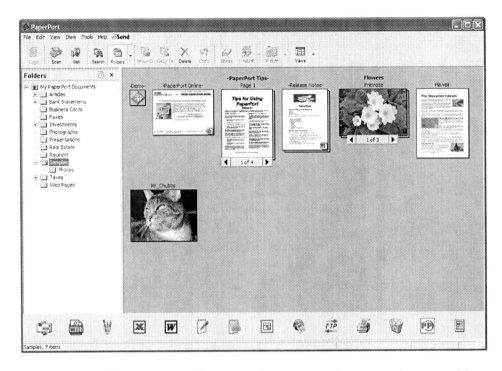

For the SOHO, PaperPort offers the ability to instantly send an item (graphic, document, and so on) to the PaperPortOnline web site, where it is stored safely using the SSL (Secure Socket Lock) which is the same software protection that guards your credit card numbers when you order online. You can send a file to your own password-protected "vault" for later viewing or for viewing by another person of your choice. Also, because the documents are stored securely, they are safer than sending via e-mail. One year of online service is included with the software, along with 25MB of online storage space.

To work on a scanned document using PaperPort's built-in OCR feature requires only a click. Just take a part of the document or the entire text, and drop it into a word processing program (Word, and so on). The OCR engine will automatically convert the scanned text into a text you can edit within that program. You can select "search" to search your files using "exact text" or "approximate" text, or by name, author, or key words.

This program also works on digital photos. Once digital photos are scanned or opened within the program, photo enhancement tools allow you to adjust the contrast, brightness, color, and tint of your photo.

Share Your Scanner

When scanners were very expensive, it was important to be able to share these valuable pieces of office equipment. Several scanners were designed to be attached to a network and shared by multiple users. As the cost of scanners fell, the need for a centralized network scanner went away except in organizations (like an ad agency) that have several stations that need to share a high-resolution scanner. Even with scanners as inexpensive as they have become, it is still good management of office assets to have several users sharing a common scanner. Allowing several users to share the same scanner can be achieved quite simply by using a USB switch. Unlike a USB hub, which allows a single computer to connect to multiple USB devices, a USB switch allows multiple USB devices to be switched between computers. For example, a four-port USB switch allows up to four computers to share all of the USB devices connected to the port.

I hope that your understanding of how versatile a scanner can be in the workplace has been enlarged. In the next chapter, we will learn how to use the scanner to do some creative projects.

8

Chapter 9

Put Your Scanner to Work at Home, Too

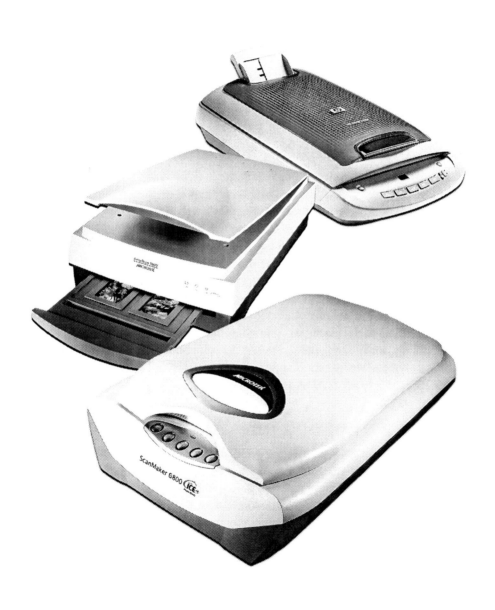

How to…

- Scan oversized pages from your scrapbook
- Stitch multiple scans into a single image
- Make a photo calendar with your scanned photos
- Search for and discover photo projects on the Internet

The number of projects you can use your scanner for at home is only limited by your imagination. You'll be glad to know that most of the projects and ideas discussed in this chapter do not require any special scanning skills. So, let's get started.

Scrap Booking—Scanning and Sharing Memories

Creating scrapbooks has become a very popular activity among the arts and crafts set in the past few years. One of my coworkers, Denise, created a scrapbook that has chronicled every major event of her daughter's life. It is a labor of love and represents many, many hours of work. Although I had heard about this scrapbook, the first time I saw it, its size surprised me. The standard scrapbook page is 12×12", and the volume she showed me was over three inches thick.

This was my first experience with scrapbooks, and I immediately saw several potential issues with her creation. Denise has poured a lot of her life into this document and has no backup copy. Scrapbooks, just like photos and other documents, fall victim to time and the elements. The other limitation is the difficulty of sharing this wonderful document with others. Sharing her scrapbook with out-of-town family members is only possible by bringing them the book. (Even if shipping costs weren't prohibitive, the thought of sending it in the mail is the stuff nightmares are made of.)

How to Get a Scrapbook into Your Computer

The solution to the two aforementioned problems would be to scan all of the scrapbook pages. Not only would scrapbook creators preserve all of their work, but they also could share their scrapbook online with friends. But how do you scan a 12×12" document when most consumer scanners have a maximum scanning area of 9×11"?

Great Places to Buy Scanners

If you ever need to buy an oversized scanner (or any scanner, for that matter), consider that most scanner companies sell refurbished versions of their scanners at a reduced cost. Another good place to buy scanners really cheap is eBay. The disadvantage of buying refurbished scanners is that they are usually discontinued products, and the warranty is much shorter than for a newer product. This isn't much of an issue when you consider that if a scanner hasn't failed in the first 20 hours of operation, it probably never will. My advice to people who buy refurbished scanners is to use them as much as possible during their shortened warranty period. Buying from eBay will typically save you even more money, but is coupled with the risk of buying from an unknown seller and getting a scanner with no warranty.

9

There are two ways to scan these large scrapbook pages. The easiest solution is to buy an oversized flatbed scanner, which scans an image area a little larger than 12×17". They are called *oversized scanners.* They used to be called "tabloid scanners" since they could scan an entire tabloid-sized sheet of paper (11×17") in a single scan. Unfortunately, these scanners are not cheap. The least expensive scanner is the Umax 2100 XL and it sells for over $1,000. Epson has two oversized scanners (Figure 9-1) that each cost several thousand dollars. So, unless you are doing scrapbook scanning as a home business, a cheaper solution is needed.

How Big Does Your Scanner Need to Be?

You can scan a 12×12" page on your home scanner if it is large enough. Consumer scanners have a typical scan area of 8.5×11.7". Because we are going to capture the scrapbook page in two separate scans, the width of the scanned area is of no concern. We are only interested in the maximum length that the scanner can scan. Business scanners, which need to scan legal-sized documents, have a larger scan area, with the typical being 9×14.5". To find out if your scanner is large enough to do the job, look in your user's manual (or go online to your scanner manufacturer's

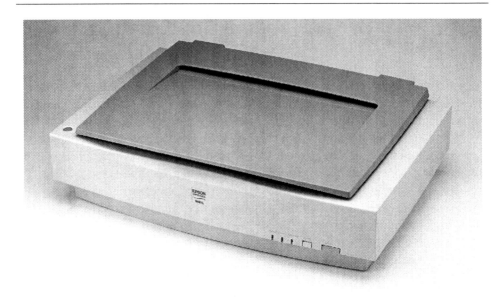

FIGURE 9-1   The Epson Expression 1640 XL is capable of scanning an entire scrapbook page in a single pass.

web site), and look at the scan area that is advertised. An example of the online specification for an HP business scanner that sells for around $400 is shown next.

Scanning dimensions

automatic document feeder	Optional, 50 sheets
maximum scan size	8.5 x 14 in ←
interface	USB (cable included; Windows 98, 2000, Me, and Mac OS only), SCSI (cable and card required)

While business scanners will cost more than really cheap consumer scanners, they still cost a lot less than an oversized scanner. On the positive side, the scanners with the larger scanning area typically are much better scanners in terms of the quality of image that can be scanned using them.

Note that although your scanner may only support scan areas that are 11, 11.5, or 11.7 inches in length, you may still be able to use it to scan your scrapbook. Look at your scrapbook and ask yourself these questions:

- Does your scrapbook go to the very edge of each page?

- If you lost a half an inch off of the top and bottom of each page, would it affect the scrapbook enough to warrant buying a new scanner?

If you answered "no" to both of these questions, your existing scanner will work for you. To prove this point, I have done the next example with a scanner that only scans to 11.5 inches in length.

How to Scan Your Scrapbook Page

Once you have a scanner, you only need one more thing, an image editor. This topic is covered in great detail in Chapter 13. Here is how to scan in the page:

1. Remove the scrapbook page from the scrapbook, and lay it face down on the scanner with the long side of the page tight against the edge of the scanner glass edge, as shown next.

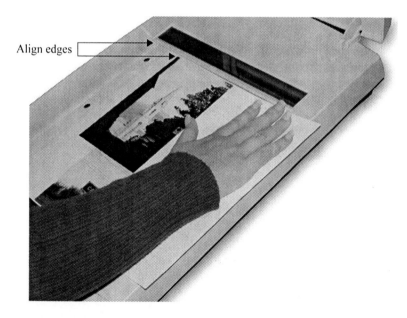

Align edges

2. If your scanner isn't as long as your page is tall, decide which edge (top or bottom) will be aligned with either the top or bottom edge of the scanner glass, and use the same edge for both scans of the page.

3. Launch the scanner software either from the image editor using the File | Import or Acquire command or by pressing the scan button on the front of the scanner.

4. When the scanner page appears in the preview window, ensure that the output is set to RGB or 24-bit color. (HP also calls this mode "millions of colors.") If the page has any printed items like newspaper clippings or photos from magazines, make sure that you set the scanner for descreen.

5. Make no selection and your scanner will scan the entire scanner glass area. Be aware that scanning this large an area will produce a large file. Scan the document. When you start the scan, your scanning software may present you with a warning box telling you that you haven't made a selection when you start the scan. Click OK and scan the first side. There may be a check box that, if checked, will prevent the warning box from reappearing the next time you scan. You will save time by turning off the warning.

6. Once you have scanned the page, save the file using a non-lossy file format such as TIFF. Do not use JPEG to save the original. Use a name that identifies the page and side, for example, PAGE01_LEFT.TIF.

7. Move the page over so the other side is tight up against the edge of the scanner, as shown next. Run a preview to ensure the page is on the scanner glass straight, and repeat the process, except change the title to **PAGE01_RIGHT.TIF**.

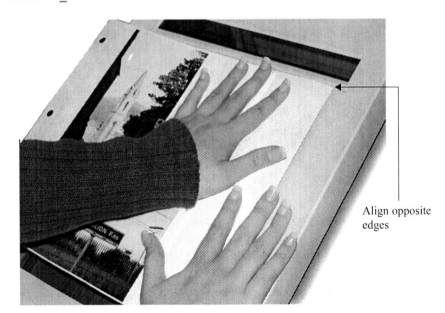

Align opposite edges

How to Stitch Your Scans Together

Now that you have scanned and saved the two sides of the page, you need to learn how to stitch the two scans together. Regardless of which image editor you are using, the procedure to make the two into a single image is basically the same. Here is how it is done:

1. Open one of the saved pages. The image that is shown next is the left side of the Halloween page.

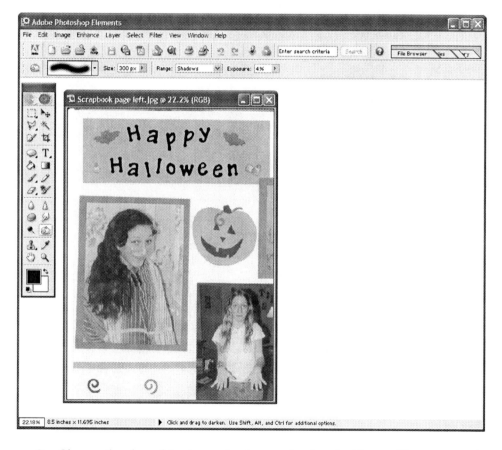

2. Change the size of the image background using the Canvas Size command in Photoshop Elements, as shown next. (Use the Canvas Size command in Paint Shop Pro.) See the Did You Know box, "The Difference Between Resize and Canvas Size Commands," to learn more about how this works.

Since the finished size of the two pages will be 12 inches, make the new canvas size a little larger so you have room to work. The new image is shown in Figure 9-2.

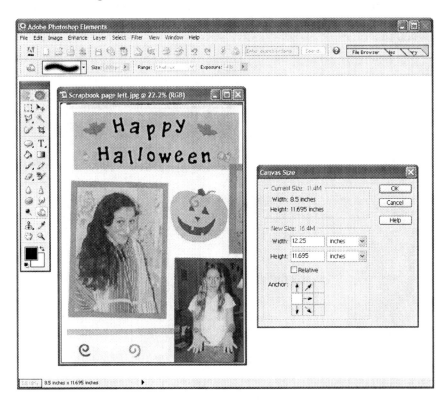

3. Open the second scanned image. Select the Move tool (V) in Elements, click inside the image you just opened, and drag the image over the first scanned image. A copy of the second image is now a layer on the first image, as shown next.

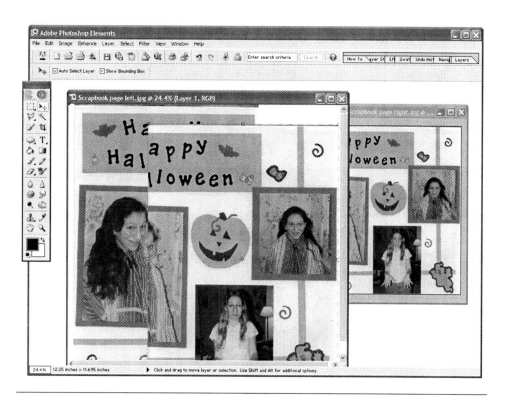

| **FIGURE 9-2** | The original left page is now large enough to fit both scanned halves of the scrapbook page. |

4. Close the second image and return to the first image to align the two layers. To make alignment easier, change the blend mode to Difference. The layer now looks like a negative, as shown next. Using the Move tool, align the overlapping edges of background and the layer. Set the zoom to 100% (Actual Pixels), and when the alignments get close, use the arrow keys to make the final adjustment. Here is a tip—they will never align perfectly; just get them as close as possible.

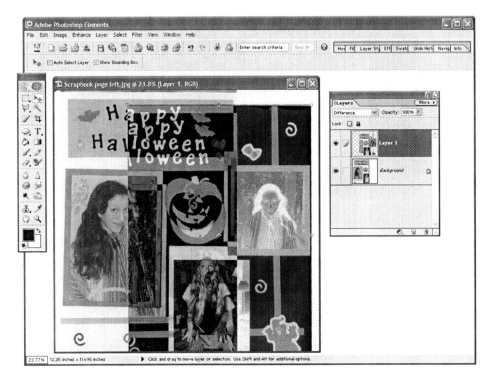

5. Once you have aligned the edges as closely as possible, change the blend mode of the layer to Normal. At this time, you will discover that the two scans will have an edge (as shown next) that is a shadow created by the scanner light.

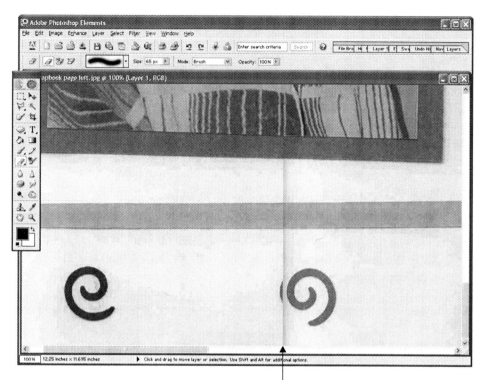

Seam between the scanned images

The Difference Between Resize and Canvas Size Commands

You can make an image larger using a photo editor application in two ways. You can enlarge the actual image, or add a border around the edge of the existing image. Using a resize command makes the image you are working on either larger or smaller by adding pixels to the image. Alternatively, a canvas command lets you add or remove workspace around an existing image. The newly added canvas background appears around the border of the existing image. With the canvas command, you can choose to add the new border material equally around the edges, or apply it off-center as was done in the previous exercise.

Regardless of what image editor you are using, they all work the same; in most cases the name of the command has the word "canvas" in it. The color of the new border is determined by the currently selected background color. By changing the background color, you can add an appealing border to a photo. The last use of the canvas command is for cropping. If you make the new canvas smaller than the original, it will crop the existing image—which is a quick way to trim an odd-sized image to a specific size.

6. With the top layer still selected, use the Eraser tool along the edge until the seam is gone. Once the seam is gone, merge the layer with the background (flatten).

7. Crop the resulting image (Figure 9-3), and use Save As to save it under a different filename.

FIGURE 9-3   This 12×12" scrapbook page was scanned on a scanner with an 8.5×11" scan area.

Share Your Scrapbook

Once you have your images in an electronic form, they are preserved, but they can now also be shared over the Internet. One way to do this is to use a program designed to display photos like FlipAlbum by e-book Systems (www.flipalbum .com). Figure 9-4 shows the image we scanned in the previous part of the chapter appearing as a page in a virtual scrapbook whose pages flip (probably why they called the product FlipAlbum). This album can be viewed online, or burned as a CD and sent to friends and relatives.

Once the scrapbook page is scanned, you can reduce its size and send it as part of an e-mail. In the example shown next, the same image was reduced to

9

FIGURE 9-4   A virtual scrapbook can be created for viewing online with FlipAlbum.

a resolution of 72 dots per inch (dpi) since it was originally scanned at 200 dpi, saved as a JPEG file, and included in an e-mail.

There are two ways in which a scanned image can be included in an e-mail: you can attach it, in which case the file format of the image can be any graphics format, or you can save it as a JPEG and actually include it in the e-mail, as shown earlier. Attachments are the preferred method if you think the person receiving the image does not use Windows. If you attach a JPEG file to an e-mail, it appears as an icon on your outgoing mail. But if the person receiving it is using Internet Explorer, the actual image (not the icon) will appear in the e-mail when the person opens it.

Scrapbooks and Copyrights

Is scanning a professionally taken portrait photo to put on your scrapbook page a copyright infringement? Yes. Yet I know people who use their portraits for all kinds of products such as mouse pad pictures, calendars, coffee cups, business cards, greeting cards, plates, papers, and family Christmas newsletters. Are they criminals? Technically, anyone who scans a professional portrait has infringed the copyright of the photographer. So, do you know of anyone who was arrested by the copyright police for making copies of a school photo for placement in their family newsletter? Of course not. However, if you decided to make a little side money by setting up shop at your kid's school and producing copies and enlargements of school photos, you might get to meet the photographer's lawyer.

Capturing Memorabilia

9

Scanners, just like cameras, are tools used to capture images. Use your scanner to create fun decorations for your pages, record small items, or both. Your child's treasures piled onto the scanner screen provide a way to capture objects that could not otherwise be placed in the scrapbook without taking a picture. You can scan memorabilia such as your child's artwork, a hand, or even a foot. But while scanning hands and feet are a great way to show how small their hands and feet once were, be careful not to damage the scanner or your children by having them stand on the scanner glass.

You can also scan memorabilia such as awards and certificates of success. For example, if you have a certificate that is too large to fit into your scrapbook, just use the controls on your scanner to scan it as a smaller image. Print the reduced image and place it in the scrapbook.

Creating Gifts and Other Projects

A wealth of free craft projects from major corporations is available on the Internet these days. Let's face it, the companies want you to come back again and again and buy their products, so they offer some pretty amazing stuff that will either make you feel good about their company or cause you to use lots of their consumable products (paper and ink) because you are making so many of these creative ideas with your scanned photos.

The Internet is a moving target. By that I mean that any web sites that I list in this book are subject to change. So for that reason, I have only mentioned a few web sites from several major companies that are market leaders and who probably won't be changing their web addresses soon.

Make a Photo Calendar

Most software today includes some sort of calendar-making program. I use the online versions since they are free and I think they're quite creative. My favorite is Hewlett-Packard's web site (www.hp.com). It takes a little navigation, but they have several great creative idea sites like the Digital Imaging Center shown next, which has a wealth of projects to do with your scanned photos (or even the photos from your digital camera).

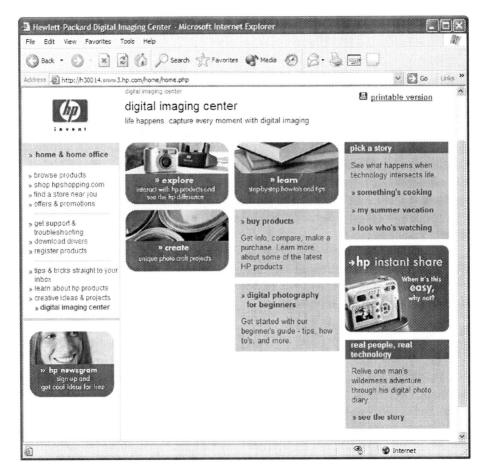

In the Cards & Stationery directory (shown next), you'll find a great selection of calendars, cards, and invitations. Figure 9-5 shows two calendars I made using some scanned photos.

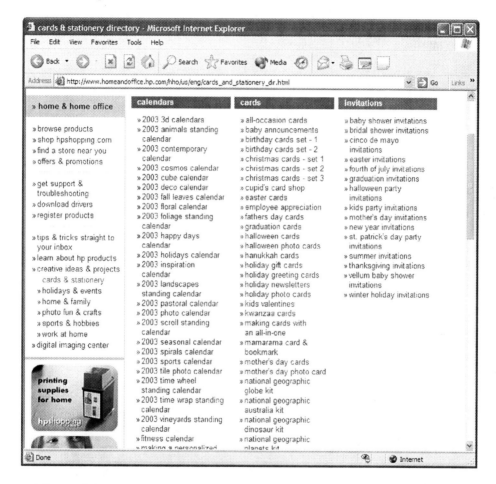

Microsoft has some great templates with which you can create some even more practical calendars in their Office resource area. Unlike the HP site, you must have either Microsoft Word or Works to use the templates in this site, but since MS Word is the dominant word processor, that includes most of you. The easiest way to get there is to open Word, go to Help in the menu, and choose Office on the Web. Or you can go to http://office.microsoft.com/assistance/. Selecting the Template Gallery opens a large assortment of templates for a variety of purposes and occasions, as shown next.

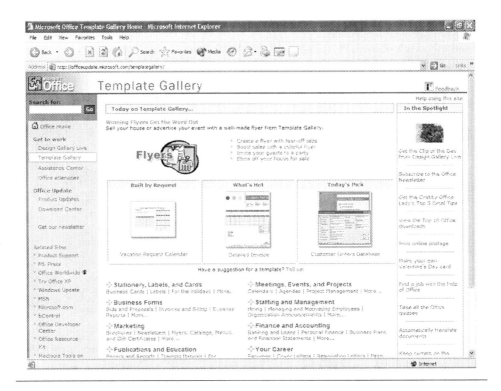

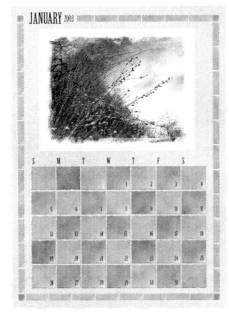

FIGURE 9-5   Here are two calendars I made online at the HP web site.

On the HP site, you upload your photos, and they place them into predesigned calendars. With the Microsoft site, you download the templates, insert your own photos, and add all of your own personal information. This gives you more control, and you can make some really great calendars like the one shown in Figure 9-6, which includes a photo of the best technical documentation team in Motorola.

You can also make T-shirt iron-ons, greeting cards, photo gift bags, baby and bridal announcements, and the list goes on and on. These are only two of the hundreds of sites that offer either free online services or templates that you can use with their software to make really cool projects.

Too Much to Cover

In this chapter, we have only scratched the surface of what you can do with your scanner and all the trappings of life that you have around your home. For more of these ideas than you can handle, I recommend using a great search engine called

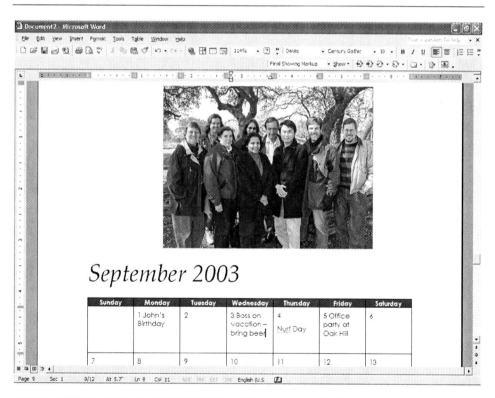

9

FIGURE 9-6   Using templates from Microsoft lets you use your scanned photos to make personalized calendars.

Google (www.google.com). Search using the words "photo" and "projects," and you will get more listings than you could view in a lifetime. To get a shorter but visual preview of the hits that Google finds, click the Images tab and see what happens.

In the next chapter, we are going to learn how to get the best possible scan and how to overcome scanning problems that inevitably occur.

Part III

Advanced Scanner Stuff

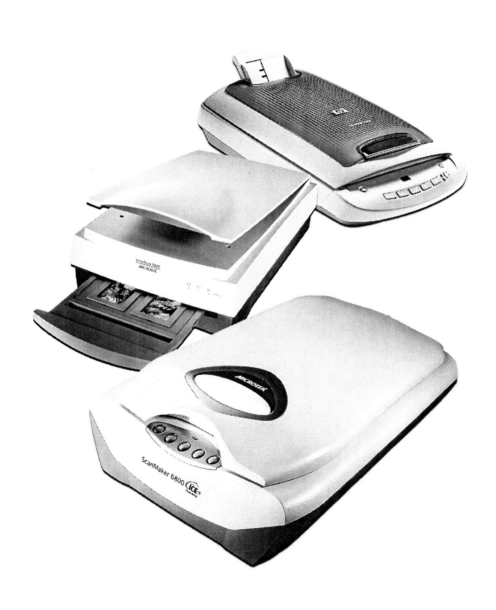

Chapter 10

Get the Best Scan You Can

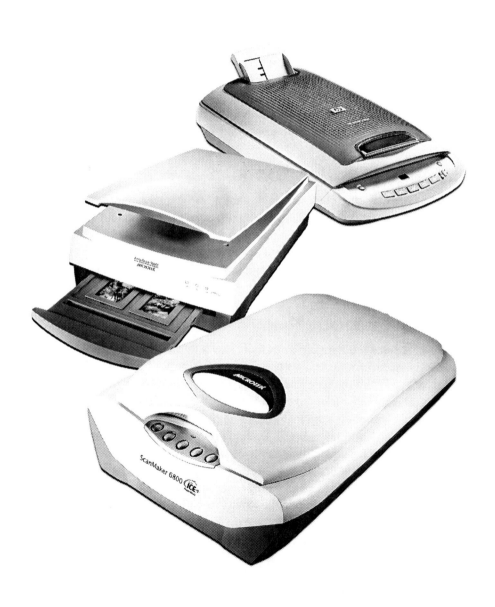

How to…

- Use the advanced features of your scanner
- Fine-tune the automatic scanner features
- Prevent bleed-through when scanning thin paper
- Scan printed material

A lot of features available in scanners today can make your scanned photos look even better than you thought possible. While each scanner manufacturer has its own approach to these features and their names, their operation is the same regardless of who makes them. In this chapter, you'll learn just what these tools are, and more importantly, when and how to use them. You will also learn how to overcome some common problems we all run into when scanning originals.

Discover Your Scanner Tools

Regardless of what scanner you own, the scanning software that came with the scanner is tightly integrated and aware of all the scanner's features and capabilities. This is why I have been recommending throughout the book that you always use the scanning software that was provided by your scanner's manufacturer rather than the featureless Windows WIA (Windows Image Acquisition) dialog box that Windows Me, XP, and 2000 provide.

Make Your Automatic Tools Work Better

Your scanner has many automatic tools built into it that analyze the image you're scanning and that make adjustments to achieve the best possible scan. Still, it is your responsibility to make sure that the image you want to scan is selected properly for the automatic tools to do their best.

When you do a preview scan and make your initial selection, like the one shown in Figure 10-1, the scanner will evaluate all of the pixels inside the selection to determine the best settings. The area inside the selection shown in Figure 10-1 includes pixels that should not be evaluated by the scanners for the purposes of setting the exposure settings. The areas that should not be included are the white background from the scanner lid and the off-white border of the photo.

The result of the selected area, including pixels that will not be in the final image, is a low-contrast scan shown in Figure 10-2 (left). If the selection only includes the subjects of the scan, the automatic exposure adjustment produces a better scan, as shown in Figure 10-2 (right).

Off-white border
on photograph

White background
from scanner lid

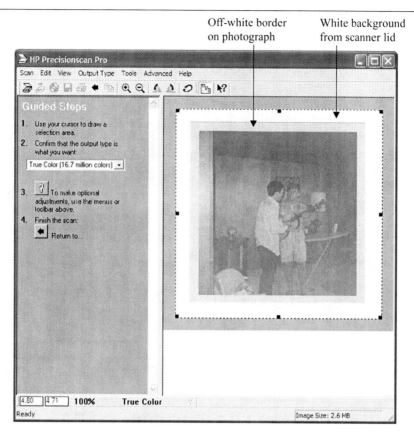

FIGURE 10-1   The selected area affects the automatic scanner tools.

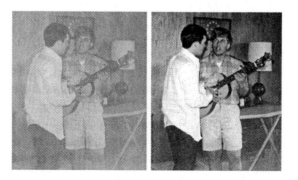

FIGURE 10-2   The selection at left includes other non-image areas; the selection at right
is limited to the image area.

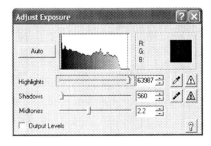

FIGURE 10-3   The Midtones setting at its initial setting of 2.2

Automatic Tools Can't Do Everything

A lot of photographs to be scanned are beyond the help of the automatic tools. To get the best scan with such photos requires an observant eye and manual adjustment tools.

Most of the manual adjustment tools for your scanner are hidden. This is because in most cases the automatic adjustments do a good job. When they don't, it is time to help the scanner out.

Adjust Exposure Manually

When the selection is correct but the image is still too dark (underexposed) or too light (overexposed), it is possible to control the exposure adjustment manually. To lighten or darken an image, we must change the midtones setting.

The midtones setting adjustment shown in Figure 10-3 lets you lighten or darken the middle values (midtones) of an image while leaving the highlights and shadows unaffected. Also called *gamma,* the midtone field ranges from 1.0 to 4.0, with 2.2 being considered the midpoint for PCs.

Moving the pointer toward 1.0 (left) darkens the image (as shown next), while moving the pointer toward 4.0 (right) lightens the image, as seen in Figure 10-4.

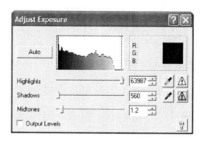

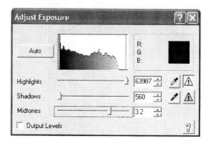

10

FIGURE 10-4   Using the gamma setting to lighten a scan

The Power of Midtones (Gamma)

Anytime an image needs to be darkened or lightened either during a scan or after the image is scanned, you should use the gamma adjustment to do it. If an image is lightened using a brightness control, all of the pixels in the image are brightened. As a result, all of the pixels that are already very bright will become pure white, and any detail that was in this area will be washed out (called a *blowout*). Likewise, darkening the image with the brightness control will darken all of the pixels, and those in the shadow region of the photo will turn solid black—again, losing any detail that might be in the shadows. When the gamma (midtones) of an image is adjusted, the pixels in the brighter and darker regions of the photo are unaffected, and only those pixels in between those extremes are affected. This allows you to make an image either lighter or darker without blowing out the highlights or turning the shadow portion of a photo into an inkwell.

Change the Midtones Setting

Here is how to change the Midtones setting using Hewlett-Packard's Precisionscan software; the setting's operation is nearly identical in the Epson, Microtek, and Canon software:

1. Choose Advanced | Adjust Exposure, which opens the dialog box shown next.

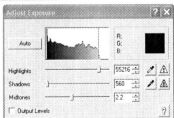

2. Move the Midtones slider either to the right or the left to lighten or darken the image.

Figure 10-5 shows the original scan that was done using automatic settings. Because of the bright sky, the scanner's automatic exposure adjustment attempted to balance the bright overcast sky with the dark shadows. The result was an overly dark photo. By manually adjusting the midtones, it was possible to recover the details in the photo, as shown in Figure 10-6.

Other Manual Adjustments

Most scanners let you make quite a few other manual adjustments. Some of the adjustments you can perform involve color (hue), saturation, and sharpening. But just because the adjustments are there, doesn't necessarily mean that you should adjust them all. Let's look at some of the more common ones.

Color and Saturation Controls

Color in an image is composed of two components: hue and saturation. *Hue* refers to the overall color of the image, and *saturation* refers to the intensity of the colors. When you change the hue, you are actually changing all of the colors in an image, not just a single color. Saturation controls how vivid a color appears. When the saturation is set to zero, the color photo appears to be grayscale (also called "black-and-white photo"),

10

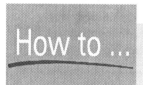 **Speed Up Your Scanning**

When you are scanning a lot of photos, one thing that will slow you down is waiting while the scanner lamp warms up. If the scanner has not been used for a while, the scanner lamp turns itself off. Also, the lamp goes through a warm-up period each time you start the software. Your scanning software usually has an option either to turn off the scanner lamp delay (not recommended since the delay ensures the scanner lamp produces an accurate color scan) or to leave the lamp on for a longer period of time than normal. If you're starting the scanning software from within a photo editor using the Import or Acquire command, you can change the preferences of the image editor so that it leaves the scanning dialog box open after the scan is complete. By default, the scanning dialog box closes after each scan. By not closing the scanning software, you don't have to constantly reopen the scanner, and the timer on the scanner lamp doesn't reset and restart the delay the next time you scan.

FIGURE 10-5   The scanner's automatic exposure sometimes gets fooled by photos.

and when it is set to a really high value, the colors become oversaturated, which can make the colors appear unreal.

It is easy to change both the hue and the saturation of a scanned photo. With the exception of using these controls to create a special effect, I recommend not changing these controls from their default settings; it is difficult (read "impossible") to accurately judge either the hue or saturation of the scanned image, because a preview scan is a low-resolution image. Another reason for not changing these values during scanning is that it makes more sense to make these changes using an image editor like Photoshop.

FIGURE 10-6   Adjusting the midtones manually improves the photo.

Sharpening—A Double-Edged Sword

Does a photo you want to scan seem a little out of focus? Do you think applying sharpening will help? Surprisingly, it may. Increasing sharpening enhances detail in the image. Most scanning software automatically selects the best level of sharpening. You might consider increasing sharpening if the original photo appears fuzzy. On the other hand, you might want to decrease the amount of sharpening if the original item has flaws or marks on it. This is because increased sharpening can make flaws stand out, or in some cases it can even create undesirable patterns.

Solve the Scanning Challenges You'll Encounter

Some items, like photographs, present few problems when they are scanned. When you start scanning printed material, like scanning the front page of your local newspaper after you've won first place in the watermelon seed–spitting contest, getting a good scan requires a little extra tweaking.

When you scan any material that is both thin and printed on both sides, you have a good chance of scanning what is printed on the back at the same time you capture what's on the front. This *bleed-through* can be a real problem, but in most cases it is easily solved. The image I scanned for the example is clipart that was printed in a newspaper. As you can see in Figure 10-7, when the clipart was scanned, the material on the other side was captured simultaneously.

10

FIGURE 10-7   The image shown here is scanned from a newspaper.

The material on the other side is captured because the paper is so thin and the underside of the scanner lid is so white. The light from the scan head penetrates the newsprint and is read by the recording head of the scanner. One way to reduce the amount of bleed-through is to put a sheet of black construction paper behind the image you are scanning. After scanning again, the results are shown in Figure 10-8. It is an improvement, but the background can still be seen.

Remove Bleed-Through Using Manual Threshold Adjust

The black-and-white threshold manual adjustment can only be applied to images being scanned as black-and-white images. Unlike grayscale images, which contain 245 shades of gray, black-and-white images, also called *line art,* have only two colors—black and white.

The *threshold* is a value in the image that defines the border between black and white. All values in the scanned image that are lighter than the threshold are converted to white, and all values darker than the threshold are converted to black. Choosing a threshold value closer to zero makes more pixels become white, while a higher threshold value makes more values appear as black.

If placing black paper under the image you want to scan doesn't work, open the threshold adjustment, and move the threshold point until the background bleed-through is no longer visible. In most cases, you can use the preview scan to come up with the optimum setting, as shown in Figure 10-9.

lunch or drinks or brunch

FIGURE 10-8   Putting a sheet of black paper behind the original reduces—but doesn't eliminate—bleed-through.

FIGURE 10-9   Adjusting the threshold setting of the scanner produces the best results.

Remove Bleed-Through with Your Photo Editor

The same threshold technique described in the previous section can also be accomplished using an image editor, which better shows the results of the adjustments than the preview scan on the scanner software. Here is how it is done:

1. Scan the image as a grayscale. The resulting image will appear softer (lower contrast), and the background won't appear to be white.

2. Convert the image from grayscale to black and white.

3. With the image open in the image editor, select the Levels adjustment (found on all image editors), and a dialog box similar to the one shown next appears. Adjust the threshold until you reach the point that is a

compromise between the background being white and detail in the foreground not being lost.

4. When you are happy with the results, change the image back to grayscale and save the file.

Scan Printed Material

When photos are prepared to be printed on a press or laser printer, a halftone screen is first applied. Without getting too technical, the screen pattern that allows a photo to be printed on an offset press is also the same pattern that develops unwanted patterns called *moiré patterns.* Most scanning software today offers a descreen command that reduces these moiré patterns in the printed items you are scanning. Another example of these undesirable patterns is the circles that often appear on pictures printed in newspapers—especially the Sunday comics.

Because of the way your scanner reduces these patterns, scanning (including the preview scan) always takes longer when the descreen command is selected.

Now that you have learned a few basics concepts about how to make better scans and scan printed materials, it is time to learn how to scan color slides and negatives.

Chapter 11

Scan Your Negatives and Slides

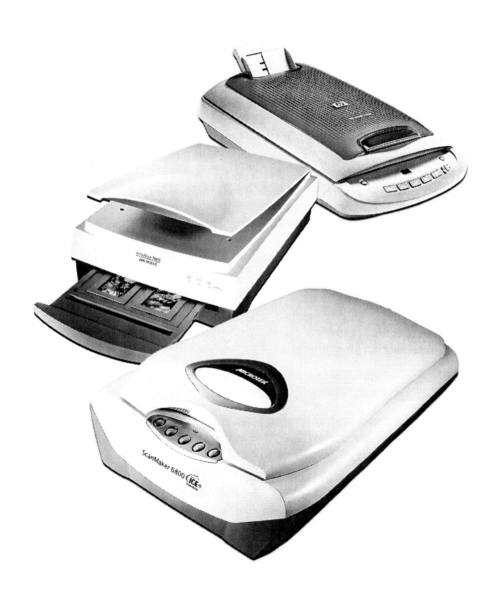

How to...

- Understand the advantages of scanning negatives and slides
- Compare film scanners and film adapters
- Select the film scanner that meets your needs
- Prepare negatives and slides for scanning

With more people owning and using digital cameras, fewer and fewer negatives and color slides are being produced. Still, there are several reasons to have the ability to scan negatives and color slides. If you are a serious photographer who has yet to switch from film to digital, a film scanner lets you continue to take pictures using film and convert it to digital images for manipulation with a photo editor. Most of us who want the ability to scan film own shoeboxes (or their equivalent) full of negatives or slides that are deteriorating ever so slowly even as you read this. Once the negatives are scanned, they are preserved and protected from further deterioration. In this chapter, we learn the advantages of dedicated film scanners and of transparency adapters for flatbed scanners.

The Advantages of Scanning Negatives and Slides

Scanning film produces superior results to scanning a print of the same subject. There are several advantages to scanning film and slides:

- Film (slide or negative) is the original image, while a print is a copy (a second-generation copy).
- Film has greater dynamic range (contrast) than can be achieved by scanning prints of photographs.
- When the photograph is printed, some tonal range is lost, and some color information is modified. This information cannot be recovered, meaning we cannot get that data back from prints.

Not that you shouldn't scan color photograph prints—just that scanning film produces noticeably better output than is possible from scanning prints. This is especially true if you plan on enlarging the image to any degree.

Color Slides Are Superior to Color Negatives

Density range is simply the difference between the minimum and maximum tonal values that the film can register. Also called *dynamic range,* it is measured in a dMax number that has a maximum theoretical value of 4.0. Negative color film has much less density range than slides. (Slides can be near 3.6, negatives about 3.0, while color prints have a dMax of about 2.0.) This means that color positives (slides) can capture a greater range of colors or tones than color negative film can. Before you run out and start shooting color film, recall the dMax number (2.0) I included for color prints. If the photo will ultimately end up as a print, it doesn't matter if you use color negatives or positives since both have a much greater dynamic range than color prints.

Choose Between Scanners

When it comes to scanning slides and negatives, you have three choices. You can use a dedicated film scanner, a transparency adapter on your flatbed scanner, or a slide copier attachment on your digital camera (slides only). Before digital cameras came along, the last option wasn't available and when it came to choosing which of the two methods to use for scanning film, there was no contest; the dedicated film scanner (Figure 11-1) was the only reasonable choice.

Flatbed scanners have seen tremendous improvements in the past few years, and with transparency adapters (Figure 11-2) it is possible to get results with your flatbed scanner that almost rival dedicated film scanners.

The choice of a scanner for scanning film and negatives is pretty simple if you follow a few guidelines:

- If you are a film photographer and scanning negatives or slides is something you will be doing on a continuing basis, you should consider a film scanner with Digital ICE technology. At the time I am writing this, you can pick up a new Coolscan IV scanner with Digital ICE[3] online for under $500.

- If you are a former film photographer who (like me) now is shooting digital cameras and has a ton of slides and negatives to digitize, I would still recommend getting a dedicated film scanner. After you load all of your slides and negatives into your computer, you can resell the scanner on eBay.

11

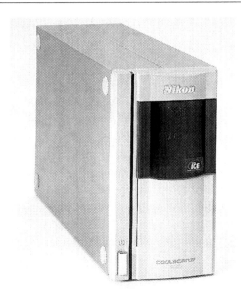

FIGURE 11-1   This Nikon Coolscan IV is a dedicated film scanner that can produce the best possible scans from your film.

FIGURE 11-2   Transparency adapters on newer flatbed scanners can produce excellent scans.

■ If your film scanning needs are occasional, you should consider getting a good quality photo flatbed scanner with a transparency adapter. A good photo flatbed will meet your film scanning requirements.

Advantages of Dedicated Film Scanners

Photo flatbed scanners with transparency adapters can produce some excellent scans, but film scanners offer a few unique features that make slide or negative scanning much easier. The primary advantage of the dedicated scanner is ease of use. The scanner, like the one shown in Figure 11-3, is designed to hold film or slides.

Slide scanners used to cost several thousand dollars (the high-end scanners still do), but in recent years the price of dedicated film scanners has gotten as low as $150.

Digital ICE—Almost Too Good to Be True

If they ever decide to add a scanner category for the Nobel Prize, Digital ICE™ would win hands down. This marvelous invention from Applied Science Fiction (yep—that's the name of the company) actually removes (rather than covers up) defects in scanned slides and negatives. The image shown in Figure 11-4 is an actual horrible negative that was scanned and had Digital ICE applied to it.

11

FIGURE 11-3   A dedicated film scanner simplifies the scanning of negatives and slides.

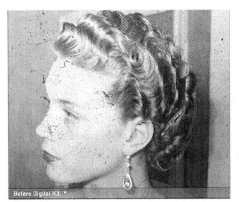 

FIGURE 11-4 The original negative (left) and the improved image (right) after Digital ICE was applied.

Digital ICE technology works from within a scanner to automatically remove surface defects such as dust and scratches from scanned images without altering the base image. Film scratches and dust that adversely affect picture quality can occur during picture taking or during the printmaking process. However, the Digital ICE technology automatically enables the film scanner to correct for these defects without degrading the image quality or slowing the scanning speed. When I first saw Digital ICE in action, I was hoping that it was software that I could install and use with my existing scanner. Alas, I discovered that the scanner manufacturer had to design a scanner specifically to use it. Initially, it was only available on a Nikon CoolScan slide scanner, but now it is available on several slide scanners, and for the first time it is available on a Microtek flatbed scanner.

The newest version of their technological magic is called Digital ICE[3] (pronounced "ICE cubed"), which adds two more features called Digital ROC™ and Digital GEM™. Digital ROC automatically restores original colors to faded slides and negatives. It reads the dye signature in color negatives and slides and restores colors to the appropriate levels. If you have old slides or negatives in which the color has faded, this program does an excellent job restoring the color—even on some of my old slides that had gone almost pure magenta.

Digital GEM reduces image grain caused by the film emulsion. Digital GEM automatically enhances the clarity of a scanned film image while preserving its colors, gradations, and sharpness. Digital GEM analyzes a film's unique grain pattern pixel by pixel; extracts all data related to image quality, color, and sharpness; and removes the grain from the scanned record of the image, which results in dramatically improved images.

The Film Has Two Faces

The first step in learning to scan or clean negatives and slides is to learn to tell the emulsion side of film from the base side. Knowing one side from another is necessary for proper scanning and for cleaning.

Hold the film up to the light and rotate it slightly. When the light hits the base side of the film, it will bounce off brightly because the base is the shiny side of the film. The emulsion is the dull side and usually has less gloss or shine to it when light is reflected off it. Although the base of any film will be shinier than its emulsion, it is sometimes difficult to tell one from the other. Another way to tell emulsion from base is to hold up a short piece of film and look at its curl. The emulsion side of the film will be on the inside of the curl. Negatives and slides are always handled by their edges to avoid getting grease and dirt from your fingers on it. Never pick up film or handle it with your fingers flat on its surface. This rule applies even when you are wearing gloves. Last point—yes, the title of this topic was a play on the movie title *The Mirror Has Two Faces.*

11

The First Step: Cleaning Negatives and Slides

Before you scan negatives or slides, they must be cleaned. In previous chapters, I have stressed the importance of cleaning images before scanning them because the later removal of dust or debris in the computer is time-consuming. A famous quote by John Wesley states that "Cleanliness is indeed next to godliness." When it comes to slides and negatives, it is fair to say that cleanliness is next to impossible. While cleaning is important with scanning photographic prints, its importance when it comes to slide and negative scanning cannot be overstated. This is because the small size of the original combined with the great degree of enlargement produced by the scanner, results in even the smallest dust specks becoming the size of small boulders.

Cleaning slides and negatives can be tricky. I say this because they appear to be natural magnets for dust and fingerprints—much as an expensive silk tie attracts soup stains. Here are some basic techniques for cleaning and otherwise preparing slides and negatives for scanning.

Canned Air or Air Compressor

Don't blow dust off negatives and slides with your breath. If you only are scanning slides and negatives on an occasional basis, canned compressed air is a good solution.

Always blow air across a mounted slide, not at it. Canned compressed air has sufficient force to blow a slide right out of its mounting.

There are several inherent problems with canned air; it costs too much, it can spit propellant onto the negative or slide, and it isn't all that powerful when the can gets half empty (or half full if you're an optimist). If you scan negatives and slides a lot, I recommend going to your local hobby or craft store and purchasing an air compressor that's used for air brushing, similar to the ones shown next.

Quite a few different kinds of compressors are available. I recommend that you avoid the compressors that look like aquarium air pumps. I also discourage the temptation to buy a complete airbrush kit since you don't need an airbrush, just the compressor and a 6–10-foot length of hose. Expect to spend between $75 and $150 (even less on eBay) for the compressor. This roughly translates into the price of 30–40 cans of compressed air. The air that comes out the end of the hose will be more powerful than what comes out of the can, and it will not spit propellant onto the surface of the slide.

How to Clean a Really Dirty Slide

Even the best air compressor cannot blow either grime or fingerprints off the color slides. I am sorry to say that while there are film solvents designed to clean negatives and slides with light dirt and fingerprints on them, none will be able to completely do the job when it comes to a really dirty slide. If the slide is really important to preserve, it will take some time and effort, but here is what you must do:

1. Remove the slide from the cardboard mount.

2. Soak it in a dish containing a solution of Kodak E-6 Final Rinse that's been warmed to about 90–100° F. You can buy a small bottle that makes a gallon of solution for around $4 at any camera store.

3. Let the slide soak in the solution. Its emulsion will swell up (it turns pasty gray in color). With your fingertips fully moistened with the same solution, gently—very gently—rub off any grit or grime from the emulsion side. Grime on the base (shiny) side will generally come off just with the primary soaking. If there are any fingerprints, the rinse should remove them.

4. Set up a string like a short clothesline to hang the individual wet slides. Open a paper clip a little so that you can insert it into one of the film sprocket holes and can hang the slide from the string. Let the film air dry.

> TIP *When drying your slides, ensure the drying area is relatively dust free.*

5. I recommend remounting the slides in quality plastic slide mounts. I usually don't recommend using slide mounts that have glass inserts in them because they often cause more problems than they solve. While they do protect film from fingerprints, they are very expensive ($1.50 each compared with 10–12¢ each for glassless plastic). The glass insert often collects and traps moisture and debris inside the mount as time passes. They're also heavy when shipped and may scratch the film if broken. Wear cotton gloves when handling fresh, clean slides. Sandwich the freshly washed slide into one of the mounts and then do your scan. Avoid the temptation to scan the slides without remounting them.

11

How to Scan Film by Using a Film Scanner

Scanning either color slides or negatives with a dedicated film scanner is pretty simple. With many flatbed scanners it is possible to use the scanner without installing the software that came with it since Windows Me and XP provide a primitive Windows Imaging Acquisition (WIA) dialog box to perform a scan.

The software that came with the film scanner must be installed to be able to scan color negatives.

1.   Clean the film and note the manufacturer (Kodak, Fuji) and the kind of film (Royal, Kodak Gold, Fujicolor Superia, and so on) and the ISO (exposure rating) of the film negative by reading the edge of the negative. For most color slides, the type is printed on the slide mounting as shown in Figure 11-5.

2.   Place the film or slide holder of the scanner as directed by the manufacturer. In most cases, it will be emulsion side down (see the Did You Know box— "The Film Has Two Faces").

3.   Perform a preview scan. The dialog box for SilverFast software used with a PF1800 film scanner is shown in Figure 11-6. Make sure the software is set for either negative or positive. Also ensure that the settings are correct for the film manufacturer, type, and ISO setting.

4.   Make sure that the output is set to the correct size, and scan the negative or slide.

Now that you know how to scan film, it is time to learn some important things about storing and handling the film.

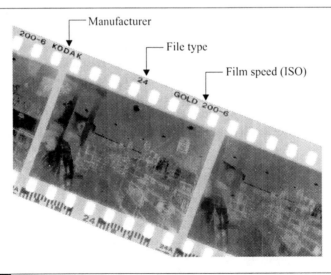

FIGURE 11-5   The information about the film is printed on the edge.

Scan Color Negatives

Scanning color negatives is much different from scanning positive slides or prints. As you may have noticed, color negatives have an overall orange mask, designed to aid photo printing of negatives onto regular photographic paper. However, the orange mask makes scanning color negatives difficult without special software.

Color negatives require that the image be inverted just like black-and-white film negatives, but color negatives also require that the orange mask color be removed by balancing it out. (It is a strong greenish blue when inverted to positive.) The software that comes with your film scanner software has a Negative mode that does this. Since the shade of orange varies among film brands, and even in different films from the same manufacturer, it is important to make sure that the film scanner software negative settings are set to the correct manufacturer and type.

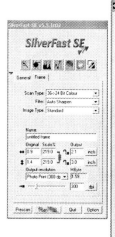

11

FIGURE 11-6   Dialog box for a film scanner

Storage and Handling of Slides and Negatives

While photos are often carefully mounted in albums, negatives are usually given
the least attention when it comes to storage. Negatives are not displayed and we
rarely look at them. The truth is, when it comes to negatives, we print them and
forget about them. Even when stored in the dark, however, color negative images
do change over time. Negatives that you intend to scan or store require a degree
of care and attention.

The most important rule is to keep negatives clean. It seems that negatives and
slides have a natural affinity for fingerprints, dirt, and dust; these contaminants
often contain chemicals that can harm the image. If you suspect that your negatives
are dirty, clean them carefully as just described before you store them.

Store Negatives Properly

What is the best way to store developed negatives and slides, for both protection
from dust and light and ease of accessibility and classification? I've found the
handiest way is to store them in special three-hole plastic sheets with pockets
(shown next) and then to put them away into office folders. Those sheets are also
quite transparent, so they can be easily looked through, as opposed to plain plastic
boxes, which seal better but are much more of a hassle to get slides and negatives
in and out of.

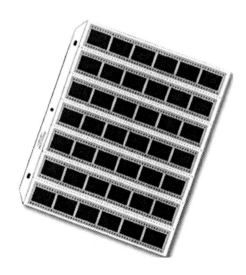

 *Use cotton gloves or handle your negatives by the edges to prevent fingerprints. The oils left by your fingers can eventually cause deterioration of the negative.*

Control Temperature and Humidity

You can store most negatives under normal room conditions. In climates where the relative humidity regularly approaches 60 percent, use a dehumidifier or other means of reducing the humidity in the storage area. (In some cases, you can use silica gel desiccants in air-tight storage containers to dehumidify.) Keep storage containers away from heat (radiators, warm-air registers) and windows where sunlight can strike them.

 *Do not store your photographic materials in direct contact with any of the following items, which can all cause acidic damage: wood, newspaper, cardboard, adhesive tapes, paper clips, and rubber bands.*

Film negatives are best kept cold. Even minor reductions from room temperature have a major beneficial impact on the stability of an image. Believe it or not, storing color negatives in a household freezer is a relatively inexpensive and reliable way to keep them for long periods. Before you chuck the color negatives in the old freezer, make sure that you seal them in moisture-proof storage envelopes to protect them. The storage temperature for black-and-white negatives is not as critical as for color negatives, but you should control the relative humidity. Those living in a drier climate should be aware that black-and-white negatives stored in an environment that has a relative humidity (RH) below 25 percent can become brittle—while my friends in Houston and the South in general have to deal with the fact that an RH above 60 percent encourages mold and fungus growth.

Things That Bug Your Slides and Negatives

Did you know that bugs can go after your slides and transparencies? Insects such as carpet beetles sometimes attack color slides and negatives, as well as unprocessed film not stored in film canisters. Don't store slides, cameras, or film in drawers, closets, or cupboards where you keep clothing or fabric, or where lint has accumulated. These materials attract egg-laying adult insects. Don't spray either the slides or negatives with a bug spray. All commercially available insecticides are petroleum-based products that will do more damage to your negatives and slides than the bugs ever could.

Before We Leave This Topic

Please don't let all of this talk about cleaning and storing negatives and slides discourage you from scanning them. When you see the difference between the results achieved from scanning a print and the negative of the same photo, you will be glad that you made the extra effort to scan film. In the next chapter, we will learn some of the techniques and tools available for storing and organizing all of the photos and other objects you have learned to scan in the last 11 chapters.

Chapter 12

Organizing Your Photos

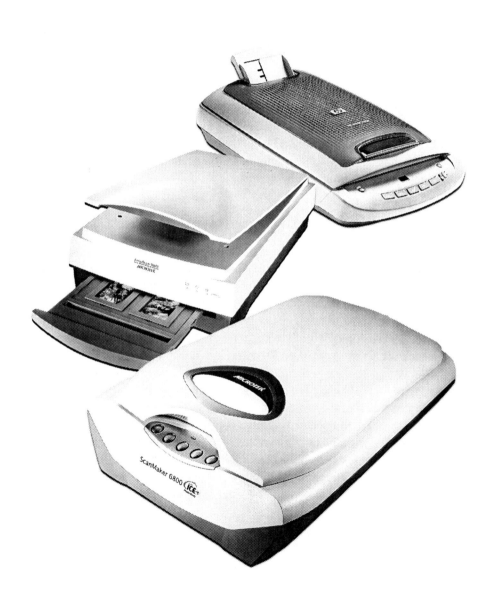

How to...

■ Discover the importance of organization

■ Compare features of different electronic photo albums

■ Decide which photo organizer is best for you

■ Organize your photo collection

The confluence of four technological wonders—digital cameras, inexpensive scanners, high-speed Internet access, and monster hard drives—has produced enormous virtual piles (more like mountains) of images in our computers. After you spend over an hour looking for a specific picture to put in the family newsletter, you come to grips with the reality of just how big your photo pile has become. Fortunately, in the past year several new and relatively inexpensive tools have appeared in the marketplace that not only help you organize your photos, but that also provide a host of other creative features.

Measuring Your Virtual Closet

If there was ever any doubt that America has a consumer-driven economy, it would immediately be put to rest by the existence of several store chains devoted to selling stuff to help you store your stuff. If I take my closet measurements to such a store, they will help me buy and install their specialty hardware to organize my closet so that I can fit even more stuff in it.

If you are like most people I talk with, your photo closet (hard drive) is a mess. Your photos are scattered on your desktop and in a dozen or more different folders, awaiting the day that you are going to sit down and organize them. I state this for readers who may think they are the only ones dealing with this mess. You are not alone. I was once told that the more creative you are, the less organized you are. If that is true, I must be one of the most creative people on the planet. The screen shot in Figure 12-1 shows the contents of one folder containing several hundred photos that were taken (by both a film and digital camera) at my niece's wedding. This doesn't show the more than 30,000 other photos I have gathered over the past 20 years. As you can see, I need a way to name, sort, and organize these photos, or I will never find them again.

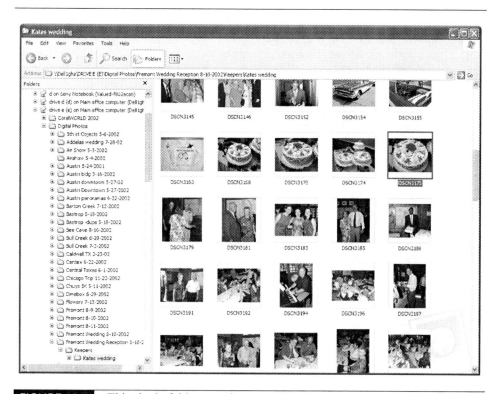

FIGURE 12-1   This single folder contains over 300 photos.

Using the Power of Windows to Organize

If you have a newer version of Windows (Me, 2000, or XP), you will notice that these operating systems recognize multimedia files and offer several tools that can be used to organize photos. For those users with small collections, these Windows tools may be sufficient to manage what you have.

Finding All of Your Photos

The first step is to find all of the photos on your computer. Here again Windows has a lot of tools to make this step easier. Here is how to do it:

1. Go to Start and choose Search. The dialog box that appears is dependent upon the version of Windows that you are using.

2. If you are using Windows XP, you can select Pictures, Music, or Video
   in the What Do You Want to Search For? section of the dialog box;
   the screen shown next opens. If you are using an earlier version,
   see the Did You Know box, "Different Ways to Search for Photos,"
   later in this chapter.

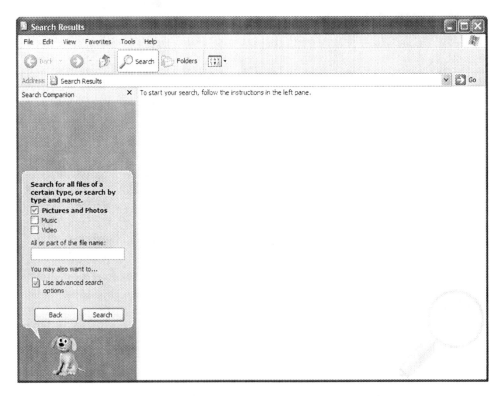

3. Checking the Pictures and Photos box and clicking the Search button
   without entering anything in the All or Part of the File Name box will
   cause the computer to search for every photo on your computer. The result
   of searching my laptop for all pictures and photos is shown in the next
   screen shot, and yes, that is 4,407 photos—just on my laptop. A couple of
   quick points. Even though I have a very fast laptop (2GHz), it still takes
   Windows some time to search all of the 30GB internal hard drive. It takes
   even longer to generate all of the thumbnails if that viewing option is
   selected.

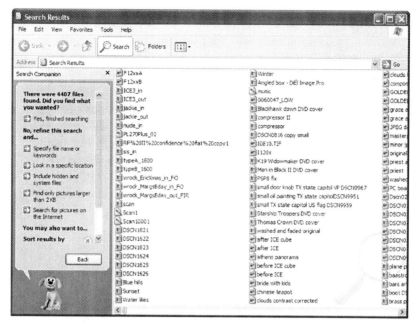

4. To move the photos to a single location, select all of them (CTRL-A) and click the Folders button in the toolbar, which opens an Explorer pane on the left of the dialog box, as shown next.

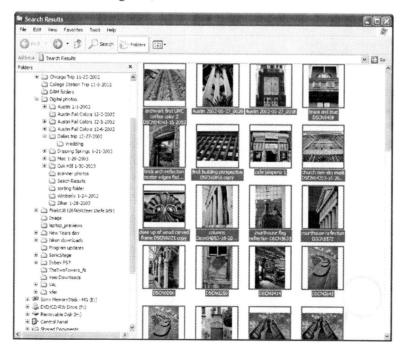

12

5. If you hold down the left mouse button and drag the selected photos from the pane on the right into the folder in the Explorer pane on the left, you will place a copy of the photos in the Explorer pane. If you hold down the right mouse button and drag them, when you release, you will have the option to copy, move, or create a shortcut (which is not related to what we are doing here). The difference between copy and move is that if you move the photos, after the image is moved to the folder, the original is deleted; whereas if you copy them, you have duplicate files in both the new location and the original location.

Different Ways to Search for Photos

The search features found in older versions of Windows are less robust and require a little more effort from you to locate all of your images. All versions of Windows have a search feature (called a *search engine*). To find photos with the earlier versions requires the use of wildcards.

A *wildcard character* is a keyboard character such as an asterisk (*) or a question mark (?) that is used to represent one or more characters when you are searching for photos or images. Wildcard characters are often used in place of one or more characters when you do not know what the real character is or when you do not want to type the entire filename of the photo or other image. Use the asterisk as a substitute for more than one character. If you are looking for all of the JPEG photos on your computer, you enter ***.JPG** (called "star-dot-jpeg"). The asterisk tells the search engine to locate every file that has a JPG extension. The question mark is a substitute for a single character in a name and isn't used as much as the asterisk when searching for photos.

The most popular formats to search for when looking for photos are *.JPG, *.TIF, *.GIF, and *.BMP. The last two formats will produce hundreds, if not thousands, of hits because so many icons in both Windows and web pages are either *.GIF or *.BMP. These are easy to sort out. See the section, "Viewing and Sorting the Search Results."

Viewing and Sorting the Search Results

Once Windows has found all of your files, you have several options for viewing and sorting them. Here's a brief guide to how to view and sort any file or image using My Computer.

Getting a Different View of Things

When you open a folder using My Computer (Start | My Computer), the contents are displayed according to the settings for the folder.

 The following description applies to most editions of Windows XP, but some vendors have customized the version of Windows shipped with their computer, and it may not work exactly as described here.

Clicking the View menu option opens a list of six viewing options:

- Filmstrip
- Thumbnails
- Tiles
- Icons
- List
- Details

Viewing as a Filmstrip

When the Filmstrip view is selected, your pictures appear in a single row of thumbnail images (Figure 12-2). This view is horizontal in its orientation, so you must scroll through your pictures using the left and right arrow buttons, or grab and drag the scroll slider at the bottom of the window. If you click a picture, it is displayed as a larger image above the other pictures. If you double-click one of the thumbnails, a separate window will open displaying a much larger version of the image.

Using Thumbnails

The view option named Thumbnails displays thumbnails of the images. For folders, the folder icon displays thumbnails of the first four images in the folder, as shown

12

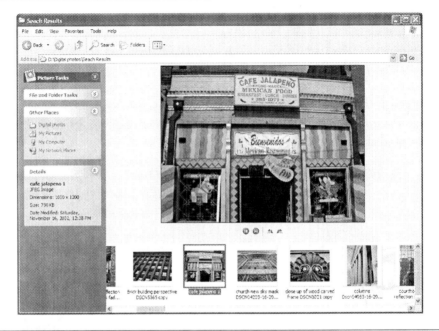

FIGURE 12-2 Filmstrip view allows you to see enlarged versions of selected photos.

next. This view is vertically oriented, so you must scroll up and down to see images and folders that are not visible in the screen.

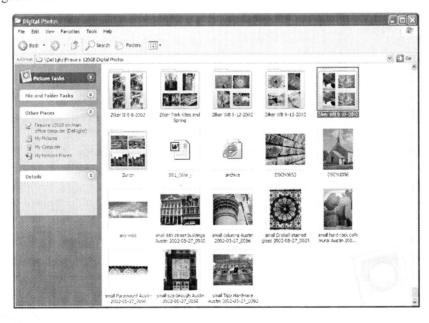

The thumbnails are displayed on the folder to help you identify the contents of the folder. While the icons might jog your memory as to the general contents of the folder, a serious downside is associated with viewing photos with the Thumbnails view. Unlike the file browsers in image editors such as Paint Shop Pro and Photoshop Elements or photo album programs, some versions of Windows do not create a *cache file* of the thumbnail images. Cache files are unique to each application and contain thumbnails of the images in the folder. Without these files, every time you open a folder containing images, the operating system must regenerate the thumbnails. Even if you have a fast system and your version of Windows does generate a cache file (as indicated by the presence of a thumbs.db file), if you have many photos, it can take a significant time for Windows to read and display the thumbnails for all of your photos.

The Tiles and Icon Views

These two views mainly differ in the size of the icons they display. The Tiles view displays your images and folders as icons like the ones shown next. The icons are larger than those in Icon view, and the sort of information you select is displayed under the file or folder name. The window orientation is vertical, so you need to scroll down to see images and folders not visible onscreen.

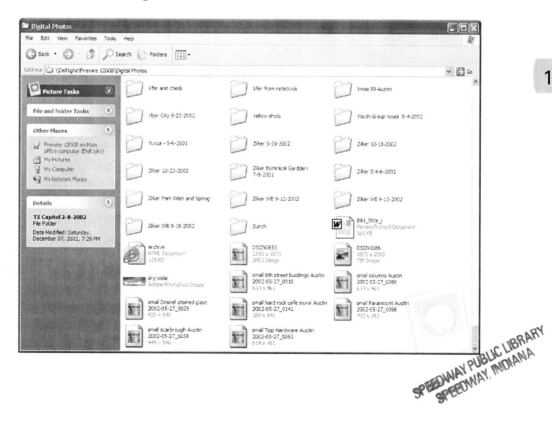

The Icon view is just like Tiles view, except smaller. The screen shown next is the same as the one shown earlier, except that with the smaller icons, more folders and images can be shown. As with Tiles view, the images scroll vertically.

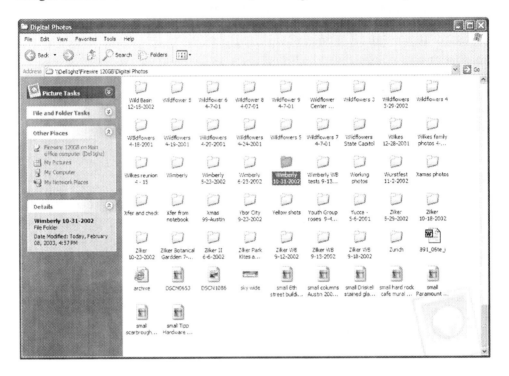

The List View

List view displays the contents of a folder as a list of file or folder names preceded by small icons. The List view has the smallest icons and the folder scrolls horizontally. The view shown in Figure 12-3 is scrolled all the way over to the right. Because most of the other viewing options are vertically oriented, the fact that this one works horizontally has misled users into thinking a folder or photo they're searching for isn't there since no vertical scroll bar appears.

Getting Down to Details

The last viewing option is the Details view. When this option is selected, the currently selected folder displays detailed information about your files, including name, type, size, and date modified. The real advantage of this viewing option is its capability to quickly jump between sorting options by clicking the title button on the the column. For example, if you click the column labeled "Type," all of the files and images are sorted by type of file, as shown next.

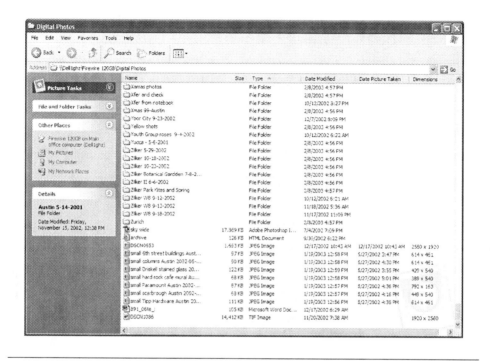

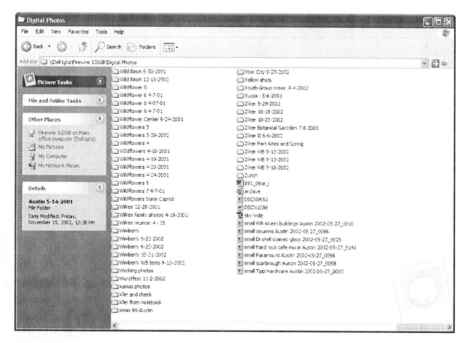

FIGURE 12-3   The List view has the smallest icons and is horizontally oriented.

How to Globally Change the Viewing Options

While you can change the viewing options of each folder as you open it, it is much simpler to decide on which view works best for you and to change them all to the same view. Here is how it's done:

1. Open a folder and select a folder view.

2. On the Tools menu, click Folder Options.

3. On the View tab (shown next), click Apply to All Folders.

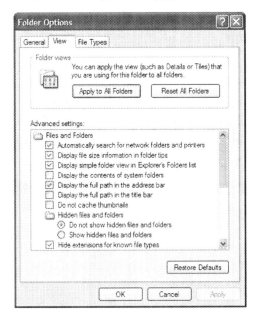

The Organization Plan

Now that you have a better understanding of how Windows views and sorts its files and folders, here is a recommendation for how to organize your images in your computer if you not going to use a third-party image-management tool.

1. Locate all of your photos.

2. If your photos are not already grouped into folders, logically divide them into folders. I strongly recommend including the event or location and date in the folder label. Examples of such folder labels are "Siberia Vacation 2003," "Aunt Jack's Wedding 1-3-1998," or "Mrs. Doubtfire's Bar Mitzvah 1-31-2004."

Did you know?

What's a Picture and Photo?

When you ask Windows to search for a picture or a photo, what is it looking for? Microsoft isn't crystal clear about what they consider a "Picture" or a "Photo," but several things are immediately apparent. Windows can recognize most standard graphics formats. For proprietary native formats like Paint Shop Pro (*.PSP), Photoshop (*.PSD), or applications that do not have a thumbnail (like Microsoft Word or Excel), the search results display the icon that represents the program associated with the file format when the folder or the Search Results window is in Thumbnail view mode.

3. If you are storing photos made with a digital camera, keep the original number assigned by the camera with the title. For example, if the photo of a bluebonnet is labeled "DSCN12345" by the camera, name it "Bluebonnet DSCN12345." This way, if you make changes to the image and at a later date want to return to the original, you can search for "DSCN12345."

Digital Image-Management Tools

12

Even if you tightly organize your collection by doing all of the things mentioned previously, if your collection of images gets large, you are going to need an image manager to keep track of all the photos. Fortunately, several excellent programs are now available that not only can sort and manage your images, but also can do other cool things.

The Power of Keywords

The way most image managers work is for the user to assign keywords to images when they are cataloged. When a particular image or group of images is desired, you enter the keywords you want to search for, and the catalog visually displays the results of that search. Figure 12-4 shows the results of a search for keywords in Adobe Photoshop Album. In this search, I looked for the keywords "Texas" and "Leaf." If you read the top of the display, there are 16 items that matched, and 3,331 images that didn't match.

You can assign multiple keywords to an image depending on what the image contains. If you are new to image managers and working with keywords, I have a

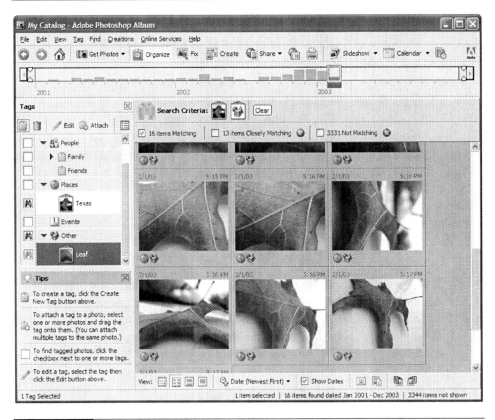

FIGURE 12-4   Image managers like Photoshop Album can instantly locate images.

few suggestions. The photo shown in Figure 12-5 is a photo of the Chicago Theater. When assigning keywords, look for words that may be used later to find it.

The obvious choices for keywords are "Chicago," "theater," "marquee," and "building." Other less-obvious choices are "exterior," "movie," and "historic." Do not aim to see how many words can be assigned, because it takes longer to catalog. Having too many words assigned can also result in excessive hits during a search. Examples of keywords that are questionable include "lights" (in the marquee), "blue," and "red" (colors in the marquee). Most image managers allow you to add keywords to a master list. Using a master list of keywords lets you check to see that you don't enter variations of the same keyword. For example, if four different keywords are used for the same subject—"grass," "grasses," "Grass," and "Grasses"—even though they're about the same subject, the search engine in the image manager searching for the word "grass" (the lawn variety) may not find them all.

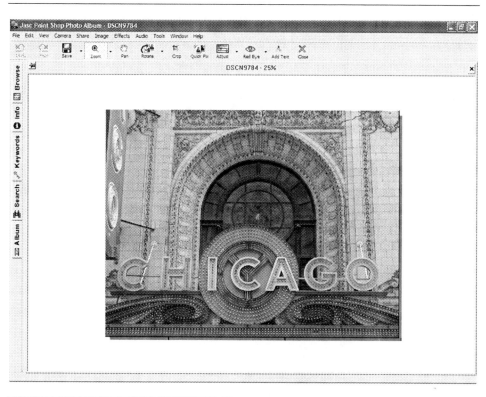

FIGURE 12-5   Choosing the best (not the most) keywords is essential to image management.

Image Management—A Lot of Choices

You can buy a lot of image managers, but there are four major image-management programs. Two of them, Jasc Paint Shop Album 4 and Adobe Photoshop Album, are new. The other two, Portfolio by Extensis and Cumulus by Canto, have been around for some time. Many shareware image-management programs, some of which have a devoted following, also are available. I am a little prejudiced when it comes to these programs. A few years back I was using one of the more popular ones to rotate some images I had in a folder. Later on, I discovered that the program had cropped the images when it rotated them—I was a very unhappy camper. With the two newer image managers costing less than $50, I can't see any reason to go with shareware. But that's just my opinion. Let's look at four programs I have already mentioned and consider the advantages of each.

Two General Categories of Image Managers

Image managers, officially called Digital Asset Management (DAM) applications though few people use that term, can be loosely divided into two categories—professional and consumer. I refer to Canto Cumulus and Extensis Portfolio as professional products because they have strong network- and file-sharing tools. The two album products are clearly targeted toward consumers—which doesn't make them any less image managers.

Canto Cumulus—A Professional's Choice

The product that has been around the longest is Cumulus by Canto (www.canto.com). It comes in three editions—Single User, Workgroup, and Enterprise—for both Mac and the PC. The single-user edition, shown next, costs around $100 and is a powerful image-management tool. But it is not the easiest program to learn how to use.

A free evaluation version is available for download. As shown in Figure 12-6, it is a full-featured copy of their program except for the limitation on the maximum number of records. Unlike the other image managers, Cumulus doesn't use the typical assignment of keywords for cataloging images; instead they use a hierarchical structure that involves placing photos into categories. The end result is the same but I just wanted to warn you about this if you use their free download

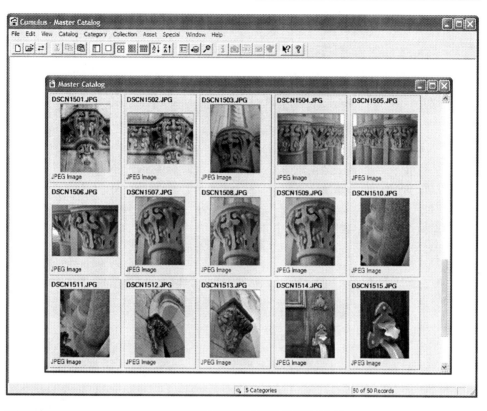

FIGURE 12-6   A catalog in Canto Cumulus displays images.

version and try to find the term keyword. The advantage of Cumulus is its powerful workflow and its network file-management capability. These features come at a price, because the Workgroup and Enterprise versions of the program plus all of the additional add-ons represent a sizable investment.

Extensis Portfolio 6

Extensis Portfolio 6 is a powerful image-management program that supports Macs and PCs. It lets you automatically create image catalogs and assign keywords en masse—a real timesaver. Once images are in the catalog, Portfolio, shown next, lets a user search by keyword, visually, or both. A feature called FolderSync allows you to move, copy, or delete files from within Portfolio and—here's the best part—Portfolio keeps track of the images so the catalog is always synchronized with the location of the actual files. This means that when the image is moved to a new location, the program is aware of it and tracks it.

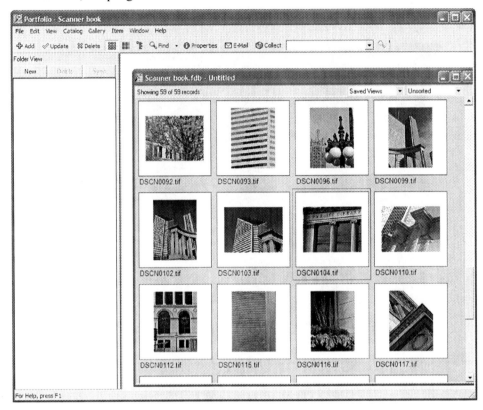

My favorite feature is the Portfolio Express Palette, which sits at the ready while you're in Photoshop (or any other application). When you need an image, you open the palette (while still in your image editor), and you have access to everything in the Portfolio catalogs. It is a very full-featured program that is in the same category as Canto Cumulus and costs $200. If you have professional needs and want a program that doesn't have a difficult learning curve, this is a good choice.

Different Programs, Same Name

A delicious irony occurred this year when Adobe announced their new image-management program named Photoshop Album almost at the same moment that Jasc announced the newest and renamed version of their image-management program, Paint Shop Photo Album 4. One of the fun parts of being an author is being able to talk with the people who work so hard to make these programs. Especially when each one discovered the other had named their product "Album." Total surprise. Back to business.

Neither program offers a Mac version, which is a big surprise, particularly for a program from Adobe. Both programs offer image management and limited image enhancement. In addition, they each have unique features that go far beyond image management. Now for the best part—they both sell for $50.

Jasc Paint Shop Photo Album 4

In addition to image-management tools, Paint Shop Photo Album offers the ability to create slideshows on video CDs that can be viewed with a DVD player, which is a great way to share photos. One of the great features in this program is an image adjustment wizard (Figure 12-7) that provides a way to improve photos with easy-to-use photo adjustment and cropping tools, and to enhance photos with special effects.

You can easily assign keywords to images with this program. After adding the keyword on the left, you only need to select the image(s) in the catalog and then click the keywords that you want to assign to the photos, as shown next.

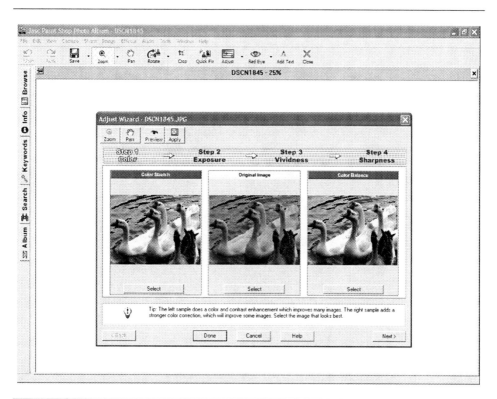

12

FIGURE 12-7   Jasc Paint Shop Photo Album provides image enhancement and image management.

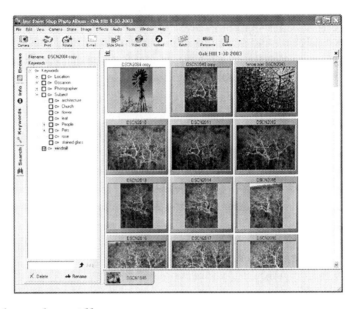

Adobe Photoshop Album

Adobe Photoshop Album is another great image-management tool that has a lot of additional features. The one feature that is unique to Photoshop Album is the timeline located below the menu bar (see next illustration). It allows you to slide the timeline to the year or the part of the year that contains the images you want.

As in Paint Shop Photo Album, the image-enhancement tools shown next can handle a goodly amount of the image adjustment and correction needs of most photos. If this program has a weak spot, the keyword capability seems limited for someone who is trying to keep track of a large number of photos. Other than that, it is really a full-featured program.

So, which one should you buy? All of them are available for download, so my recommendation is to try them and see which works best for you.

Now that we have looked at image management, in the next chapter we will learn a lot about the image editors.

Chapter 13

Selecting and Using Photo Editors

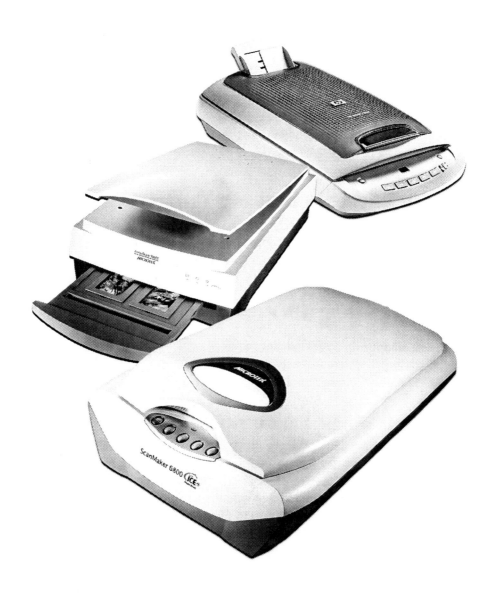

How to...

- Evaluate the differences between photo editors
- Select the best photo editor application for you
- Understand common photo editor and scanner tools
- Read and evaluate a histogram

No matter how good your scanner is, it is just an input device that, if properly used, faithfully reproduces the original photograph or image you are scanning—warts and all. After you have done all that you can do with your scanner, you can accomplish the rest of the job of making your scanned images appear their best by using a photo-editing application. In this chapter, we will look at some of the more popular photo-editing programs that you can use with your scanner and their relative advantages and disadvantages—if any.

Which Photo Editor Is Best for You?

In this chapter, we'll briefly look at the top five of possibly 30 of the most popular applications in the marketplace. Just because your editor isn't mentioned in this chapter doesn't mean it isn't good. Conversely, because a photo-editing program is in the top five doesn't necessarily mean it is the best. With the exception of the Microsoft Picture It! applications, you can download evaluation copies of all these programs, allowing you to see which works best for you.

If you are satisfied with your current photo editor—keep it. While a different program may appear more appealing, take into account the time it will take you to learn how to use a new program.

Photoshop Is King—But Do You Need a King?

When it comes to photo-editing programs, the industry standard is Adobe's Photoshop. This is the program of choice for professional photo editors and illustrators for creating, adjusting, and correcting photographs and other images both real and imaginary. Tasks that can be accomplished with Photoshop range from simple color correction of photographs to commercials and films that feature animals talking and exhibiting human movements and actions. Photoshop (Figure 13-1) is a professional

The Difference Between an Image, Photo, and Bitmap Editor

The major difference between these applications is the name. They are all, by strict definition, bitmap editors. Whether you call it a photo editor or a bitmap editor, the program does the same thing; it manipulates image pixels. Some image applications have unique features that are designed specifically for working with digital cameras and photographs. Even with the extra features, these programs can still rightly be called image editors.

program that also features a professional price tag. At this writing, the current version of Photoshop is selling on the Internet for around $600.

Until a few years ago, Photoshop was the only real choice for quality photo-editing. A few other programs offered tools similar to those found in Photoshop, but the consumer really didn't have much choice in this regard.

13

FIGURE 13-1   Photoshop has become the industry standard.

Pros and Cons of Photoshop

The advantages of using Photoshop are many. The following lists just a few of the benefits:

- Over 100 books in print about Photoshop cover a wide range of topics. If you can't find a Photoshop title that describes what you want to do with the program, you aren't trying.

- Many classes, conferences, and workshops explain how to use Photoshop.

- Many companies offer products for use with Photoshop.

The principal disadvantage of Photoshop is its cost. Another potential problem that faces many new Photoshop users is that the program can be a little intimidating to learn.

Is Photoshop Right for You?

This is an easy decision. Two categories of people should or will use Photoshop. Graphic professionals such as illustrators, photographers, and others must use this program since it is considered the standard of their business. Regardless of how good and full-featured another photo-editor application may be, many service bureaus and other organizations will only accept work done with Photoshop. It's not fair, but that is just the way it is. The other category is composed of those folk who always buy the best or most expensive product regardless of whether they need it. If you don't fall into either of these categories, we will next look at some excellent alternatives to Photoshop that don't cost more than your computer.

Many Alternatives to Photoshop

A large number of programs considered to be photo editors are in the marketplace today. It would be impossible to list them all, so I have listed the top (based on market share) four photo editors other than Photoshop. At this writing, they are (in order of largest market share):

- Photoshop Elements

- Picture It! Digital Image

- Paint Shop Pro

- PhotoImpact

Photoshop Elements

As the name implies, Photoshop Elements (shown next) is a version of Adobe Photoshop without the high price tag. The first time I became aware of the existence of Elements, I assumed it was a limited version of Photoshop—I was wrong. It is a version of Photoshop that is optimized for the digital photographer or semiprofessional graphic illustrator.

13

Most of the important tools of Photoshop that are necessary for photo editing and retouching have been retained in this low-cost version, including plug-in filter support. (Plug-ins are explained later in this chapter in the section titled "Photoshop Plug-in Filters.") What isn't in Photoshop Elements are tools necessary for doing prepress work, that is, support for CMYK images, support of vectors and paths in an image, and many others. In my opinion, Elements is more powerful than the average image editor bundled with digital cameras or scanners. You can use Elements to capture still images from a variety of video formats, including QuickTime, MPEG, AVI, and Windows Media. Like its big brother, Photoshop, Elements gives the ability to browse through thumbnails, which include a preview of the image as well as its size and type.

Inputted images can be enhanced, distorted, corrected, or combined into panoramas (Figure 13-2) through Elements' built-in PhotoMerge stitching tool. Elements also works well as a file manager, its new batch processing feature allowing users to make the same changes to several images. Output options are many, including automatically

FIGURE 13-2   This panorama was made from several photos using Photoshop Elements.

resizing and attaching photos to e-mail messages with a single click, printing images, or saving them in a smaller web format and then uploading them to the Internet. Beyond these typical tools, Elements users can create image slideshows in PDF format that can be viewed on PDAs as well as on other PCs.

This program sells for around $100 and with rebates or other promotional offers can generally be obtained for around $70. A full-featured evaluation version that will work for 30 days can be downloaded from www.adobe.com at no cost. At this time, Photoshop Elements 2.0 has been on the market for about six months, and the original Photoshop Elements program can be obtained online pretty cheaply, which is a good thing if you are really on a tight budget, since the differences between the original release and version 2.0 aren't that significant. About 35 books are in print for Photoshop Elements, including my book *Adobe Photoshop Elements 2: 50 Ways to Create Cool Pictures* (shameless plug).

Pros and Cons of Photoshop Elements

The advantages of using Photoshop Elements are many. The following lists just a few of the benefits:

- Many of the tools in Elements are the same tools as in Photoshop.

- Elements accepts most Photoshop plug-in filters.

If there is a disadvantage to this program, I haven't figured it out. I do miss a few of the Photoshop tools/commands that are not available in Elements, but other than that, this is a great value.

Microsoft Picture It! Digital Image

The version of Picture It! Digital Image Pro 7.0 (shown next) is the latest and most advanced version of a family of Picture It! image editors. Microsoft introduced the application several years ago and has worked hard to position the product in the marketplace. There are three versions of this program. If you need just a minimum feature image editor to remove red eye from photos or to create a simple photo album, Microsoft has two junior versions of the program—Picture It! Photo ($35) or Photo Premium ($55). The version of the program with the most features is Picture It! Digital Image Pro 7.0 (although you won't see the "7.0" on the box), and it includes the standard photo-editing features, like being able to remove red eye; adjust the brightness, contrast, and sharpness; crop down to a specific area; and so on. As with Photoshop Elements, built-in filters can be used to apply painterly effects like pencil, charcoal, and watercolor, and Photoshop plug-ins are supported.

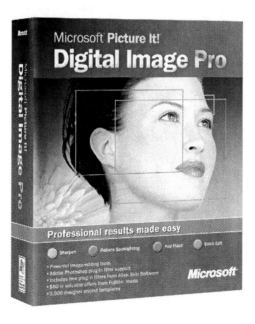

At this writing, only one third-party book is available for this program, and it is the only one of the four photo editors we are looking at in this chapter that doesn't have a downloadable version to try out. The reason it is number two in this market is because it's made by Microsoft...'nuff said.

Pros and Cons of Picture It! Digital Image Pro 7.0

The major disadvantage is that you can access almost no third-party books and few web sites for support or ideas. This shortage combined with the lack of a downloadable evaluation version make Picture It! Digital Image Pro 7.0 the least attractive choice of the editors we're looking at in this chapter.

Jasc Paint Shop Pro 8

Back when the only image editing programs were large and expensive, Paint Shop Pro (PSP) began life as a shareware program created by a Minnesota company named Jasc. The program became so popular that it wasn't long before Jasc decided that it **could** release the program as a retail product. Over the years PSP has gathered a **huge** user base and has become one of the most popular image-editing packages in **the** world.

As I am writing this, version 8 is in beta testing. PSP features include auto-enhance, which adjusts color balance, brightness, saturation, and hue to improve picture quality with a single click. It also has filters for noise, scratch, and dust removal, and automatic red-eye removal. Paint Shop Pro has vector-based drawing tools that allow the user to create shapes and other elements that are resolution independent (which means they will always look sharp and crisp when they are printed).

Its cost is in the $100 category, and you can download a free evaluation copy from their web site at www.jasc.com.

Pros and Cons of Jasc's Paint Shop Pro

Like Elements, this is a really popular program that is used for a wide variety of applications. Because it has been around for so long, it offers more web sites with creative ideas and tutorials than you can count. The following lists just a few of the benefits:

- Since it isn't genetically related to Photoshop, Paint Shop Pro has a large assortment of unique built-in photographic filters not found in other image editors.

- Over 24 books are in print about the product, including my book *How to Do Everything with Paint Shop Pro 8* (yet another shameless plug).

- Of all the editors in this price range, Paint Shop Pro has the greatest number of web sites dedicated to the product.

- Paint Shop Pro accepts most Photoshop plug-in filters.

Like Photoshop Elements, this program has almost no downside. Download the program and play with it, you'll love it.

Ulead PhotoImpact 8

Ulead PhotoImpact 8 is a consumer-oriented photo editor that has most of the bells and whistles found in the other photo editors, including support of plug-in filters. This program has a lot of interesting and creative features. It also includes several auto- enhance features for common adjustments such as focus, contrast, brightness, hue, saturation, and tones. It, too, has a long history in that the company that made it created one of the first programs that tried to challenge Adobe Photoshop. Ulead continues to improve this program with each release. PhotoImpact (shown next) sells for around $90, and you can download an evaluation copy from www.ulead.com.

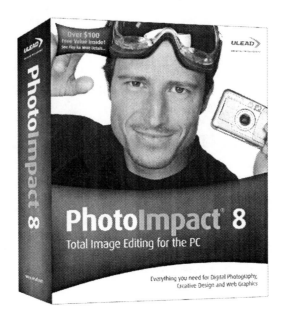

Pros and Cons of Ulead's PhotoImpact 8

PhotoImpact 8 continues to improve with each release, but it is an image editor that is still trying to catch up with the Adobe and Jasc products.

- It has some imaginative and unique filters not found in other programs.
- There are seven third-party books about using the product.
- It accepts most Photoshop plug-in filters.

The one limitation of this program that needs to be mentioned is its limited ability to work with large image files. It gets real sluggish when working on image files that are larger than 5MB, so if you will be working with large images or are using a digital camera that has an image sensor that is greater than 3MB, you may want to consider either Jasc's Paint Shop Pro or Photoshop Elements.

Photo Editing Tools and Concepts

Regardless of the image-editing program that you use, they all have tools, terms, and techniques in common. Most of the tools found in the image editors are also found in and work the same as their counterparts in your scanning software. In the following sections we will learn about these, and in Chapter 14 we'll show how to use them to make your scans look even better. We will begin with one of the most important tools—the Crop tool.

The Power of the Crop Tool

Generally, people don't think about cropping their scanned photos because of the misguided feeling that we want to keep everything that's in the photo. The truth is, most photographs are greatly improved by removing part of the scene that distracts the viewer. Cropping is done either when the image is scanned (the best time) or by using the Crop tool; its operation is pretty obvious. The part that requires judgment on your part is what to crop and what to leave. Figure 13-3 shows how cropping can improve a photograph.

Crop tools are almost universal in the way they operate. The equivalent of the Crop tool in your scanning software is the selection made during the preview. After

13

FIGURE 13-3   The composition of the original photo (left) is improved (right) using the Crop tool.

selecting the tool, you drag diagonally to create a rectangle that incorporates the area you want to preserve, as shown next.

Crop selection lines

At this point, you can use your mouse to move the lines that define the cropped area until they are in the position that you want. Many of the programs that I have worked with darken the area outside the cropped area so that you can see how the resulting crop looks, as in the preceding photo. Usually, double-clicking or pressing ENTER completes the crop, and pressing ESC cancels the operation. In the next chapter, we will learn more about ways to evaluate a photo and improve the composition of the photo with the Crop tool.

Isolating Areas of a Photo

One of the great features of photo-editing programs is the tools that allow you to select areas to which effects and corrections are applied. No equivalent scanning tool exists. These tools range from the creation of simple geometric shapes like circles and rectangles, to custom irregular shapes, like your Aunt Petunia. While each image-editing program has its own jargon to describe its specific tools, most of them employ terms used in Adobe Photoshop.

The tools used to define an area are called *selection tools,* and the area they define is called a *selection.* The area created by a line composed of a series of black-and-white flashing dots, commonly referred to as "marching ants," is more correctly called a *marquee.* The area outside the selected area indicated by the marquee is protected from any effects that are applied to the image. In Figure 13-4, I made a square selection and inverted it and then painted over it with an air brush tool in Paint Shop Pro 8.

If everything in our world were geometrically shaped, image editing programs would only need selection tools that made circles and squares. In the real world, shapes are much more complex. To make these irregular-shaped selections, you can use *freehand selection tools.* These tools allow you to make selections like

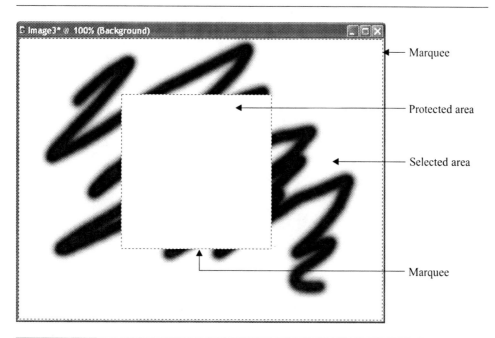

FIGURE 13-4   The area outside the selected area is protected from effects.

13

the ones shown next. The bride was getting excellent reflection off the brick wall of the church, but I ended up with a bunch of children in the overexposed background. With the freehand selection tool, I created a selection around the bride.

Freehand selection marquee

Selections not only allow you to isolate parts of a photo to selectively apply effects and tonal adjustments, but also enable you to copy selected areas and paste them into another or the same photo as a layer to make a composite image like the one shown next. In this example, the favorite priest of the bride (left) was cut out of a photo and combined with the bride to produce the composite shown on the right.

Using Image Adjustment Tools

Regardless who makes your image editor, there are two general categories of image adjustment tools—tonal and color—though they won't be called that. We will learn more about the color adjustment tools in the next chapter. The tonal adjustment tools include the following:

- Contrast (includes Auto Contrast)

- Brightness

- Histograms (also called Levels, which includes Auto Levels)

- Curves (also called Tone Curves)

Contrast and Brightness

These tools are almost always paired together, and they work on an image the same way they work on your scanner and on your computer monitor. They are simple to use but their usefulness is limited—which sounds very Zen.

Brightness affects all of the pixels in your image identically. If I have an image like the one of Mary (shown next) that is badly backlit, increasing the brightness will make every pixel in the photo brighter—even the ones that shouldn't be made brighter. Details that are lost in the shadow become more visible, but detail in the normally or overexposed areas of the photo is lost when all of the pixels become solid white (called a *blowout*).

When we talk about *contrast*, we are referring to the difference between the dark and light pixels in an image. When you scan a photo that has low contrast (sometimes called a *soft image*), the visual difference between the light and dark pixels isn't much, and so the image appears a little lifeless, like the one shown next.

By using either the scanner or an image-editing program to increase the contrast, you can make the dark pixels darker and the lighter pixels brighter. This adjustment can, when applied in small amounts, make a photo look a lot better, as shown next.

13

The danger of applying too much contrast is that detail is lost as the shadows get darker and the white areas blow out. Figure 13-5 (also a color insert) on the left shows a photo of Barbara, a tireless worker in a children's program. This photo shows several things to avoid. First, rubber chickens and pigs make poor fashion accessories. Almost as important is the application of excessive contrast (right) that results in the loss of detail on the rubber chicken (blowout) and the shadow areas as shown.

Using Histogram-Based Tools and Curves

Both of the adjustments described earlier are caller *linear tools*. They are classified as linear because they affect all of the pixels in the image the same way. But many times when working with photos, you may want to make darker pixels brighter but not change any other pixels. Tools that do this are classified as *nonlinear tonal adjustment tools*. To be able to use them effectively, we need to know a little about a scary looking device called a *histogram*.

Blowout   Detail lost in shadows

FIGURE 13-5   Excessive contrast can cause image detail to be lost.

Learning to Read a Histogram

What's a histogram? It is a method of showing the total tonal distribution in the image. It's as if your scanner or image editor were to take a census of all of the pixels in an image and then produce a bar chart of every shade of brightness in the image. Figure 13-6 shows the histogram of an image in Photoshop Elements. Histogram-based adjustment is also available with most scanner software, like the adjustment dialog box from the HP Precisionscan software, shown next.

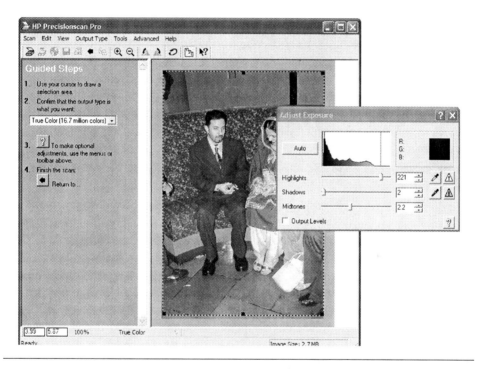

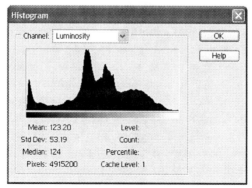

FIGURE 13-6 Example of a histogram

Brightness and Luminance Are Different

Earlier I told you that histograms display the distribution pixels based on their brightness. The truth is, histograms display the *luminance* (not the brightness of pixels). What's the difference? Luminance is a measure of the way the human eye perceives the brightness of different colors. Our eyes are marvelous devices that are more sensitive to some colors and less sensitive to others. The luminance measurement compensates for the human eye to produce a value representing the perceived brightness to a human rather than the brightness calculated from the mathematical summation of the brightness value of the pixels. So, now you know the difference between brightness and luminance. Some in the graphic arts business take great issue over this area of distinction. In my opinion, this fact you have just learned, when combined with a dollar, will get you a cup of coffee at any fast-food restaurant (assuming they charge a dollar for a cup of coffee). Feel free to use the terms interchangeably— it's a free country.

If your initial reaction to histograms is that they are way too complicated, they aren't—they only appear to be. We experience complicated visual displays all of the time without realizing it. When you see some of the stock reports on the news, they have similar charts containing even more data, but with all of that, you are only interested in one thing: Is your stock up or is it down? We are going to learn how to view histograms in the same simplistic way, and discover that they can be very useful tools.

Learning the Anatomy of the Histogram

Every pixel in a digital image has a luminance value between 0 and 255. This means that each pixel regardless of its color has a possibility of being represented as one of 256 different shades of brightness. (See the Did You Know box, "Brightness and Luminance Are Different," to learn more about luminance and brightness.) The histogram graphs the pixel count of every possible value of luminance or brightness where 0 is black at the left (shadow) end of the histogram and 255 is the white (highlight) at the right end of the histogram. The height of each vertical bar in the histogram simply shows how many image pixels are in each shade of brightness. Here are some sample photos and their histograms to make things clearer.

Figure 13-7 shows a well-balanced image displayed in the Histogram Adjustment dialog box of Paint Shop Pro 8. Pixels are evenly distributed in the three regions of the histogram (shadows, midtones, and highlights). The small arrows below the histogram are called *black point* (left), *gamma* or *midpoint* (center), and *white point* (right). Notice that in the Paint Shop Pro dialog box the three adjustment pointers are labeled "Low," "Gamma," and "High." Regardless of the name assigned to them, they act to control the tonal range of the image. We will learn more about how they work in the next chapter. Below the bar chart on many histograms (like the previous one shown) a lot of statistical data is displayed in an image editor's histogram (not in the scanner version). While data may appear intimidating, it is really easy to deal with it—ignore it. It has valuable information for prepress professionals, but you don't need it. Now that we know the parts, let's learn how to read the bar chart.

NOTE   *Having even tonal distribution of pixels in an image doesn't mean that is a good photo; it just means that it contains a wide range of image shades.*

The next photo (Figure 13-8) is one I took of an abandoned telegraph pole. Since there are only dark and light pixels in the image, with few (if any) shades in between, the histogram (shown on the right) only shows a single area of tonal distribution.

13

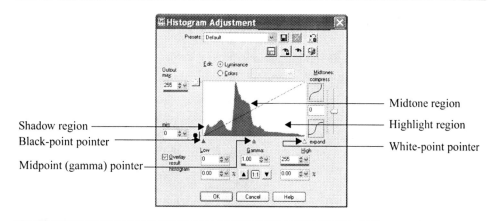

Shadow region
Black-point pointer

Midpoint (gamma) pointer

Midtone region
Highlight region
White-point pointer

FIGURE 13-7   The histogram indicates a well-balanced distribution of tonal information in the photograph.

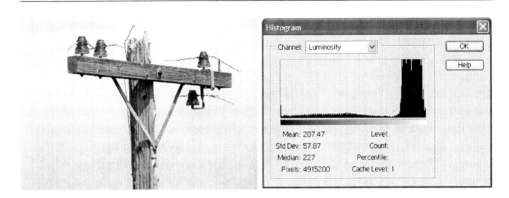

FIGURE 13-8   The histogram shows pixels concentrated in a single area.

Understanding What the Histogram Says

If the only thing that could be learned from the histogram is whether an image is underexposed or overexposed, then it wouldn't really be worth the effort to look at it. Let's look at some examples of what can be learned from interpreting the histograms.

The Importance of an Image's History

When working with digital images from an unknown source, I always recommend looking at the image's histogram to see if it has previously been manipulated. This is critical when it comes time for you to apply effects and/or enhancements to the image. If an image has been previously modified (this doesn't include rotation or cropping), it is less able to accept additional adjustments. Doing so produces visually unpleasant results like *artifacts* (small localized distortions that appear near areas of high contrast) or *posterization* (banding of colors). This is especially true of an image that has been sharpened (indicated by lots of tiny thin spikes along the length of the histogram curve). Applying additional sharpening to such an image will create unacceptable levels of noise in the final output.

When working with a photograph that you didn't scan, the histogram will tell you if the image has been modified since it was scanned or otherwise imported into your computer. Figure 13-9 is a scanned photograph taken in Chicago. The histogram adjacent to it is relatively well distributed, but more importantly, the curve on the histogram is smooth.

After applying Auto Contrast and some mild sharpening to the image, the histogram appears different, as shown in Figure 13-10. You will notice the appearance of tiny spikes along the curve. This isn't bad, it just indicates that the image has been manipulated or that it was scanned on a poor-quality scanner that generated a lot of noise. (Noise appears as tiny multicolored specks in the image.)

While You Can't Do Much With A Scan Produced By A Noisy Scanner, It Is Important To Know If An Image Has Been Previously Manipulated—See The Earlier Did You Know Box, "The Importance Of An Image's History."

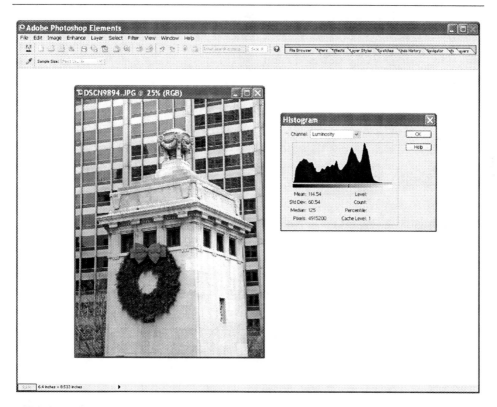

13

FIGURE 13-9 An unmodified image has a smooth curve to the histogram.

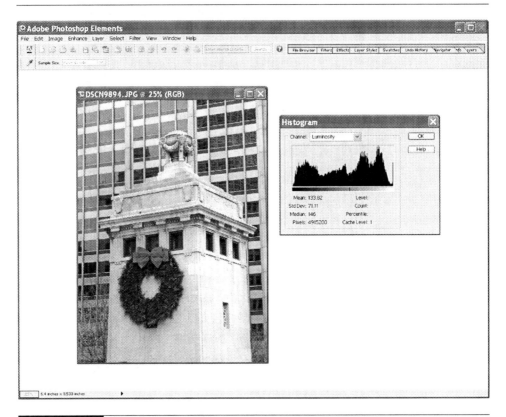

FIGURE 13-10   Application of tonal adjustment and effects produces a change in the histogram.

Other Things Histograms Can Reveal   While histograms are great indicators of the overall health of an image, they can also tell you if detail in an image can be extracted from the shadows. In the histogram shown next, you will notice that the shadow portion of the curve (left side) goes up flat against the edge of the left side of the histogram instead of gently sloping on the left side, as did some of the other histograms we have seen.

When the graph runs into the edge (either shadow or highlight end of the graph), it is called *clipping.* It tells you that there are many pixels in the image that are either pure black or pure white (blowout). If a lot of the image pixels are in the shadow region but with not a lot of clipping, there is a good chance that the image detail in the photo can be recovered. What about the highlight portion of the curve? I didn't mention this because, unlike the shadow region of the histogram, you can see the details (though they may be washed out) in the highlight region. In the next chapter, you learn how to use histogram-based tools to extract the detail from the shadow region and also how to salvage mildly overexposed images.

Understanding the Curve Tool

The curve tool exists in most photo editing software and scanning software. It is the tool of choice to quickly and easily apply tonal changes to an image. The histogram provides a strong visual of the condition of an image and the histogram-based tool—Levels—but it is difficult to control color with it. The curve tool (if your photo-editing software supports it) provides a great way to apply or remove color casts and to correct mildly overexposed or underexposed images. This is the one tool missing from Photoshop Elements 2 that I miss a lot.

Whether you are using the curve tool (which may have different names depending on the application being used) with your scanning software or with an image editor, both work the same way. The tool displays a graph (Figure 13-11) of the transfer

13

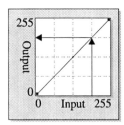

FIGURE 13-11   The curve tool appears simple, but it is a powerful tool.

function (response curve) that maps the scanner or image input tone values (along the bottom scale) to the corresponding output tone values (on the left scale). When the scanner reads an input tone value on the bottom scale, it maps it to an output tone value on the left scale, as dictated by the transfer function graph. That isn't as complicated as it sounds. By bending the curve, this tool selectively remaps the tone (brightness) of the pixels coming in to either the same level of brightness or to a different level of brightness depending on the curve created.

To explain the concept of how the curve is used, this example shows a curve that was dragged upward to brighten a slightly overexposed photo. The black arrows show this curve was moved horizontally at the midpoint (with the mouse), so the middle point data is now at the 1/4 mark. This is the same effect as in the histogram when we move the midpoint 128 to be at half that, 64. You can see that the input point at 25 percent luminance is transformed to 50 percent luminance at the output. We have lightened the shadows region while not blowing out the highlights area.

Up until now we have been studying about applying the curve function to the RGB Channel, which is a composite of RGB. We can also apply the curve to only one channel—just Blue or just Red. For example, to diminish the bluish casts that digital cameras tend to produce on bright sunny days, adjusting the curve of the Blue channel to darken just the lightest shades leaves the darker blues and the other colors unaffected. We'll learn more about actually using both the histogram levels and the curve tool to solve specific photo problems in the next chapter.

Photoshop Plug-in Filters

Whether you are using Photoshop or not, most of the image editors discussed in this chapter offer support for Photoshop plug-ins. Also called *plug-in filters,* these are third-party programs that range from utilities that make repetitive tasks easier, to wild and fanciful special effects that look fantastic—like the one from Auto FX (Figure 13-12) that makes a photograph appear to be a puzzle. Adobe gets the

FIGURE 13-12   A plug-in filter from Auto FX makes a photograph look like a puzzle.

credit for designing this feature into Photoshop way back when. Photoshop and all of the other image editors that support Photoshop plug-ins allow third-party software products to work with the image editor. If there is a downside to these plug-in filters, it is that most of the good ones are designed with the pocketbook of a graphics professional in mind and can therefore cost several times more than the hundred or so dollars you paid for your image editor.

Here are two things to consider before buying one of these special-effect wonders:

■ *Do you need it/will you ever use it?* A little company called Flaming Pear (www.flamingpear.com) makes a wide assortment of plug-ins. One of them lets you create realistic-appearing planets; another gives you the ability to make a scene appear to be flooded. The question is, how often do you need to make a spare planet or two, much less flood it?

13

■ *Will it work with your image-editor?* Most of the applications listed in this chapter work with any Photoshop-compatible plug-in. Check with the plug-in company's web page to be sure. Also note that a few (very few) plug-ins can only work with Adobe Photoshop since the plug-in is dependent on some tool or command that exists only in Photoshop.

In this chapter, we have learned about some of the image editors that are available and how their tools work, as well as a few image-editing basics. Let's see how we can use these tools to solve everyday problems with our photographs.

Chapter 14

Correct and Enhance Your Scanned Photos

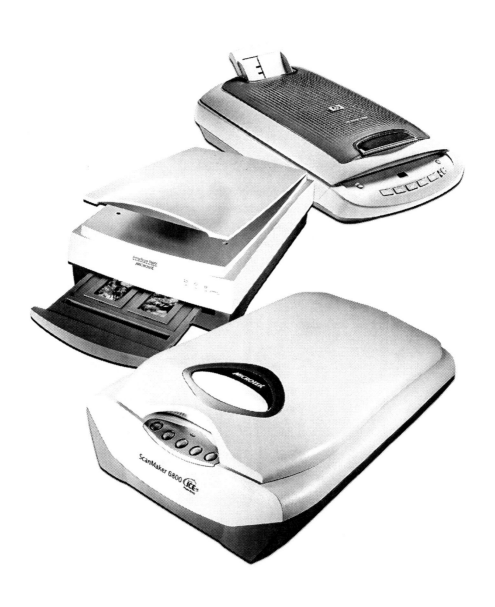

How to…

- Make enlargements of photographs
- Correct colors and remove color casts
- Remove red eye and other problems
- Sharpen a photo

This chapter explains how to use an image editor to perform minor corrections and then how to enhance the photographs so the subject actually looks better than it did when you took the picture. Whether the photo is under- or overexposed, faded with time, or the subject appears demon possessed because of red eye, you can do a lot to improve it by using the combination of your scanner and an image editor.

How to Make Photos Fit the Frame

Frequently, the photo frame that looks the best may be too large or too small for the photo that you want to place in it. A scanner feature that is often overlooked is its ability to resize an original photograph. While most of the time we want enlargements, sometimes we need to make an image smaller to fit into one of those clever precut mattes like the ones shown next.

Enlarge Photos with Your Scanner

Using your scanner to enlarge a photo is pretty simple. By default, your scanner wants to make the scanned photo the same size as the original, so making it larger requires a small setting change. Here is how to do it:

1. When you start the scan, either from within your image editor or by clicking a button on the front of the scanner, it might launch a no-frills automatic mode, which may or may not allow you to change the settings. For example, with the CanoScan scanning software shown in Figure 14-1, a button at the bottom right of the opening dialog box allows you to switch between Simple (automatic) and Advanced (manual) mode.

2. The original 4×6" photograph being scanned is of Lane, his grandson, and his son Scott. It is a good photo of them, but the three of them are lost in a cluttered background. I have cropped the preview scan as shown in Figure 14-1

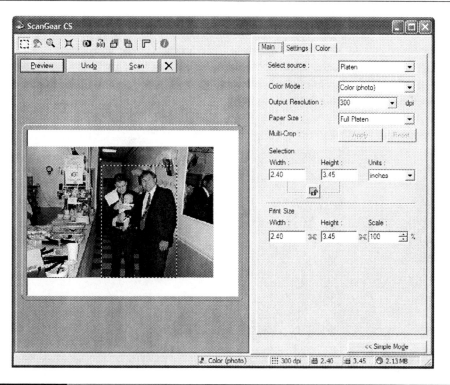

14

FIGURE 14-1   Because the subject is lost in the cluttered background, we need to both crop and enlarge.

for two purposes: to eliminate as much of the background as possible, and to ensure the resulting scan has the correct aspect ratio of a standard-size photo.

3. By changing the settings in the Print Size section of the dialog box, I am able to get pretty close to a standard 5×7" size. How you make it come out correctly is explained later in the next topic, "How to Get the Right Output Size."

4. Click the Scan button and depending how the scanning software was launched, you may have the option to save the image and open it later with your image editor. Or, if you launched the scanner from your image editor, it will scan the photo and put it into your image editor. There you can do some final cleanup, like blurring the remaining background before printing, as shown in Figure 14-2.

How to Get the Right Output Size

As mentioned in the previous section, by default your scanning software scans at 100 percent, meaning that the selected area in the preview window will not be enlarged or reduced. To get it to enlarge or reduce the image being scanned, you must delve a little deeper into your scanner software. To change the settings so the finished size is what you need requires a little footwork—or mouse work.

Figure 14-3 shows the same photo we used earlier, but this time it is on an HP scanner using their Precisionscan software. Here is how you can make the selected area into the desired standard photo size.

FIGURE 14-2   The original 4×6" photo (left) and the same photo cropped and enlarged to 5×7" (right)

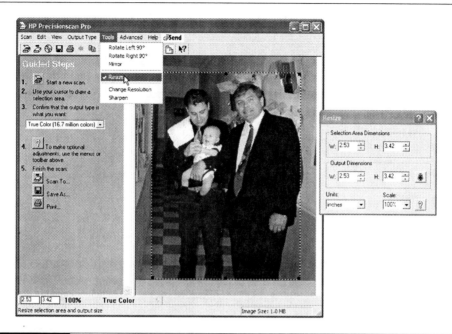

FIGURE 14-3   The Resize dialog box in the HP scanning software shows many options.

Did you know?

You Can't Make a Silk Purse out of a Sow's Ear

In the previous procedure, I showed how to scan a small area from a 4×6" photo and enlarge it to a 5×7" version. Always consider the overall quality of the photo you are scanning. In the previous example, the original I used (a color photo taken with a disposable camera) was poor. There are limits to what can be accomplished when enlarging an image, regardless of how good your scanner is. If the quality of the original is marginal, then making it larger will just magnify whatever is wrong with the photo. In most cases, you will not be able to correct these deficiencies with your image editor. In short, "you can't make a silk purse out of a sow's (pig) ear, y'all," a favorite expression of my Texan mother.

14

How to Produce Scans in Standard Photo Sizes

Nothing is sacred about the size of a photo. You can make them any size and aspect ratio that you want (see the Did You Know box, "Understanding Aspect Ratios," later in the chapter). But when it comes time to print the photo and put it in a standard frame, you discover that frames and photo paper come in only a limited selection of sizes. The more popular sizes are

- 3.5×5"
- 4×6"
- 5×7"
- 8×10"

After you have selected the portion of the photo that you want to scan, odds are that the selected area is no longer a standard photo size or aspect ratio. Here is how to ensure that the final output size that is printed fits a standard photo size:

1. After performing the initial preview scan, select the area of the photo that you want to be in the final image, as shown next.

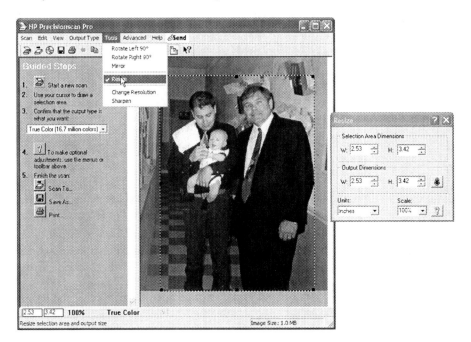

2. When you have the area selected, click the Zoom tool, and the scanner will perform another scan filling the preview window with the area you have selected. Make the final adjustment to the selection area by moving the selection lines with your mouse.

TIP   *With most scanning software, dragging the corners of the selection lines changes both horizontal and vertical selection at the same time.*

3. With HP Precisionscan software, select Tools in the menu and click Resize, which opens a separate dialog box. If you are using Epson or CanoScan, make the changes described in the next step to the settings in the Print Size section of the dialog box.

4. To make the scan fit into a photo that will fill a 5×7" frame, you must replace the longest value in the appropriate output dialog box with the longest desired dimension. In this case, it would be 7 inches. Because the Aspect ratio is locked (see the Did You Know box, "Understanding Aspect Ratios"), entering a value in one of the boxes automatically changes the value in the other box, and the scaling percentage will also change.

TIP   *In most scanning software, changing one value will not change the second dimension value until you actually click the second dimension value.*

5. At this point, you must move selection lines in the preview window until you get close to the desired size in the output dialog box. Because of the digital accuracy of the scanning software, you will find that the resulting settings may not be perfect. For example, if the output size appears as 5.01×7.01", it is as close to the standard 5×7" as you could hope for. It would be a waste of time to try and get it any closer. The final image is shown in Figure 14-4.

14

FIGURE 14-4   The cropped area produces a finished 5×7" image.

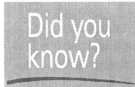 **Understanding Aspect Ratios**

Aspect ratio used to be a rarely used or understood term. Now that widescreen televisions have become popular, aspect ratios are becoming part of the consumer techno jargon. The relationship between the width of an image and its height is known as its *aspect ratio,* and from the early days of film (starting in the late 1890s) until the early 1950s, almost all movies had a standard aspect ratio of 1.33:1. In other words, the film image was 1.33 times as wide as it was tall. (Another way to denote this is "4×3," meaning 4 units of width for every 3 of height.) The term is also used to describe the dimensions of a display resolution. For example, a resolution of 800×600 has an aspect ratio of 4:3. In all cases, aspect ratio is specified as the width followed by the height. When resizing images (either with a scanner or an image editor), the aspect ratio is usually locked by default. This means when one dimension is made larger or smaller, the other dimension is increased or decreased by a proportional amount. If you unlock the aspect ratio and resize only one dimension, it will distort the image.

Resize a Photo with an Image Editor

Changing the output size of a photograph by changing its resolution is called *scaling* or *resizing.* Since it does not add or remove pixels from the image, scaling doesn't degrade the picture. All photo-editing programs offer the ability to change the sizes of images. To demonstrate this feature, I will show how it is done in Photoshop Elements.

 *Before you perform any manipulation on an image, you should always save the file so you will have the original to return to. Using the Save As command, make a copy of the image, and do all of your work on the copy—not the original.*

Use Photoshop Elements' Resize Image Command

Resize an image in Photoshop Elements by using the Resize command. With an image open in Elements, choose Image | Resize | Image Size. This opens the dialog box shown next.

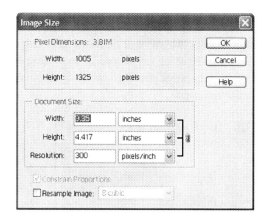

Everything you need to do to resize an image can be done from this dialog box. Now, if this is your first time seeing the Image Size dialog box, it might appear a bit complicated. Let's concern ourselves with the parts that interest us at the moment. First off, you'll notice that it is neatly divided into sections. The top section tells us the width and height (in pixels) of the selected photograph. It also shows the uncompressed size of the file—we'll talk more about compression later in this chapter. The next section shows what the dimensions of the photo are if printed at a resolution of 300 dpi. The bottom of the dialog box controls how the resizing is done.

Most of the time the only parts of this dialog box that are of any concern to most users are Resolution, Width, Height, and Resample Image. At this point, let's learn how to use this dialog box and learn a little about resolution while we are doing it.

Figure 14-5 is a photo I took of our children (Jon and Grace) at a friend's wedding. It should be pointed out that one of the advantages of being an author is the ability

14

FIGURE 14-5   Meet Jonathan and Grace; this photograph demonstrates that we have good-looking kids.

to insert photos of family and friends as examples. The Image Size dialog box (Image | Resize | Image Size), shown next, tells us that the image is moderately large—3.81MB. The size information displayed is how large the image file is after it has been opened. The actual size of the file on the disk drive is usually smaller—especially if the file is compressed.

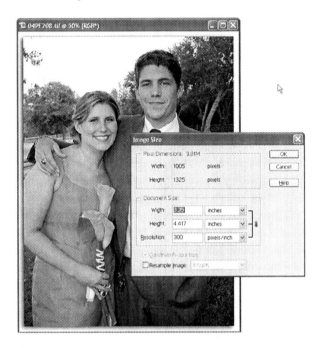

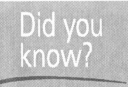

Ppi and Dpi Are Not the Same

The terms *ppi* (pixels per inch) and *dpi* (dots per inch) are frequently used interchangeably, by professionals and amateurs alike. While wrong, this isn't a problem since we usually know what we're talking about. To be absolutely accurate, you should be aware that scanners, digital cameras, and computer monitors are all measured in ppi, while printers are measured in dpi. I just wanted you to know the difference.

The Best Way to Resize

When resizing an image, the best way to do it is by changing the resolution. Choosing this method doesn't add or remove any pixels and therefore prevents any degradation of the image. This is accomplished either by unchecking the Resample Image check box in Elements or by using the Actual/Print Size portion of the Resize dialog box in Paint Shop Pro to enter the new values.

Both programs do the same thing; that is, changing the resolution causes the document size values to change, but the pixel dimensions remain fixed. For example, if the resolution is halved from 300 dpi to 150 dpi, the dimensions double even though no new pixels were added. This demonstrates a fact of image resolution: if the resolution decreases, the physical size of the output image increases. The apparent size of the image displayed in your image editor doesn't change. Why? Because the physical dimensions of the photograph (measured in pixels) haven't changed, only the resulting image size when it is printed or placed in another program has changed.

Resampling—The Other Way to Resize

The second way to resize an image is to resample it. Resampling involves having the computer add or remove pixels from the image to make the requested size change. By its very nature, resampling degrades an image. This doesn't mean you shouldn't do it; most of us who edit photos resample all the time—it just isn't our first choice. Another factor that influences resampling is whether you are making the image larger or smaller. Technically, it is called *upsampling* and *downsampling,* but I don't hear folks using those terms much any more. When you make an image smaller, there is a perceived increase in sharpness. To demonstrate this principle, the next time you go to your local appliance superstore, check out the TVs. Compare the same picture on a 32" and a 24" monitor, and the smaller image will appear sharper or more vivid. Back to resampling.

To change the size of an image using resampling, check the Resample Image box in Photoshop Elements, or use the Percentage of Original part of the Paint Shop Pro dialog box.

With either setting selected, changing any of the dimensions to fit your needs and your image editor's will add or subtract pixels from the image and the resulting new dimensions or file size. When you click the OK button, the size of the image displayed in Elements changes because pixels were either added or removed.

TIP   *If you need to resample an image, avoid increasing the size, because adding pixels tends to make the image appear soft and slightly out of focus.*

14

Straighten Crooked Scans

Some scanned images that you work with will be crooked. If you are doing the scanning, stop, lift the lid on the scanner, use the techniques we described Chapter 3 to properly align the photo on the scanner glass, and scan it again. If you don't have the original photo, then you can use your image editor to straighten it. I took the photo of Christy shown next and deliberately placed it on the scanner glass crooked.

Choices in Straightening Photos

You have several choices when straightening a crooked image, depending on the program you are using. There are automatic and manual tools. The manual method is pretty obvious; you select either custom or arbitrary (Photoshop) rotation and manually rotate the image until it appears to be straight.

Some image editors like Photoshop Elements offer automatic tools to straighten an image when you choose Image | Rotate. The two choices appear at the bottom of the pop-up list: Straighten Image and Straighten and Crop Image. Figure 14-6 shows what happens when you choose Straighten. The photo has a dark edge, which provides a strong visual reference for the vertical and the horizontal, so the program does an excellent job of straightening the photo. Because we didn't ask the program to crop the image, we are left with a large border (composed of the current background color). Figure 14-7 shows the result of Straighten and Crop Image. The program automatically detected the edges and cropped the image; though it appears to have a gray border, it is cropped to the edges.

FIGURE 14-6   Auto straightening works well with images that have dark edges.

Correct Underexposed (Darker) Photos

Darker photos tend to lose details in the shadows. Modern cameras, both digital and film, are pretty good at calculating the proper exposure so that many typical underexposures are avoided. Sometimes a scanned photo appears darker than the original photo due to a scanner with a poor tonal range. More times than not, the darkness is caused by the automatic exposure feature of the scanner being misled by a dominantly bright area of a photo. Whatever the cause, correcting the lighting of the photo with a photo editor is relatively simple. Figure 14-8 is a good example of an underexposed photo.

14

FIGURE 14-7   Straighten and Crop Image produces a finished image in a single step.

FIGURE 14-8   This brass band is a classic example of an underexposed image.

While many image editors offer tools to automatically adjust the lighting, sometimes they actually make the image worse. Here is how to correct the lighting in an underexposed photo using Photoshop Elements:

1. Open the image and then select the Levels tool (CTRL-L), which opens a complicated-looking dialog box. Position the Levels dialog box so that you can see your photo, as shown next.

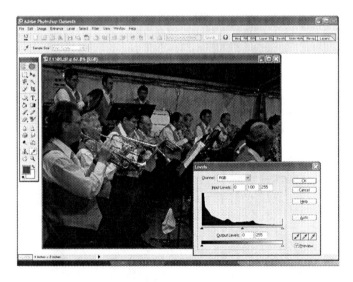

2. Change the View to Actual Pixels (ALT-CTRL-0) so that you are looking at the image without any distortion caused by the zoom function of the display.

Depending on the size and resolution of your display, parts of the image may be off the screen.

3. With the Channel set to RGB, drag the midpoint (gamma) pointer to the left until the darker portions of the image are light enough, but the light areas are not blown out, as shown next.

4. Click OK and then change the View back to Fit on Screen (CTRL-0). The result is shown in Figure 14-9.

14

| FIGURE 14-9 | Making a simple gamma adjustment using Photoshop Elements takes the band out of the dark. |

What Makes an Underexposed Photo?

The principal cause of underexposed images is that the subjects are too far from the camera for the flash to properly expose them. The flash on your camera has a limited range. This fact is discovered after a night football game when the zealous fans discover that the flash photos they took from the stands are composed of the overexposed backs of the fans that were standing in front of them and a large dark area that should have been the field. Generally, the range of your camera's flash is around 12 feet, but each camera varies. You actually should read the brief manual (most really are brief, they only appear thick because they are printed in a dozen languages), and see what the range of your camera is. Beware of getting too close to your subjects as well, or you'll either temporarily blind them or completely wash out all their features in the resulting photo.

Correct Overexposed (Lighter) Photos

Overexposed photos present their own set of problems. As a general rule, it is easier to pull detail out of the shadows than to recover detail from washed out photos. It can be done, but it is a little tricky.

Figure 14-10 is a faded photo of me and my dad that was taken in 1968. If you look at the original in the color insert of the book, you will discover that the color is faded and washed out. Using Paint Shop Pro, here is how we can restore this image.

FIGURE 14-10   An overexposed photo that has faded over time

1. Open a copy of the photo you want to work on. Select the entire image (CTRL-A), and then copy it to the clipboard (CTRL-C).

2. Paste the contents of the clipboard onto the original photo as a new layer (CTRL-L). Now we have two copies of the photo, one floating on top of the other, as shown next in the Layer palette to the right of the photo.

NOTE *If you were doing this in Photoshop or Photoshop Elements, you would paste in the new layer by using the standard Windows Paste command (CTRL-V).*

3. In the Layer palette, select the layer that was just added, and change the blend mode by clicking the word "Normal" and selecting Multiply from the pop-up menu. The photo becomes a little darker, as shown next. For more information on blend modes, see the Did You Know box, "What Blend Modes Are," later in the chapter for more information.

14

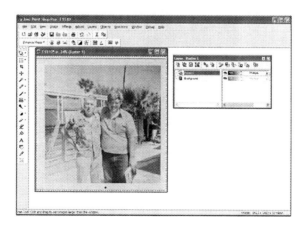

4. Paste in another Layer (CTRL-C), and change its blend mode to Multiply. Now the photo has become too dark, so clicking the Opacity setting (to the right of the eye icon) and reducing the opacity of the top layer allows the fine-tuning of the last layer and produces an acceptable photo, as shown next.

5. Once the image is the way we want it, the Layers should be flattened (Layers | Merge | Merge All) to greatly reduce the resulting file size. Save it. The result is shown in Figure 14-11 and in the color insert of this book.

The use of the Multiply blend mode cannot darken or restore detail in an area of a photo that is completely washed out.

FIGURE 14-11   It only takes a few steps to restore overexposed images into acceptable ones.

What Blend Modes Are

Blend modes control how pixels on one layer blend with the pixels on the layer (or background) below it. You use layer blending modes to determine how the pixels in a layer are blended with underlying pixels on other layers. By applying specific blend modes to individual layers, you can create a wide variety of special effects.

For example, in the previous technique we used the Multiply blend mode to darken an image. Here is how Multiply works. The image editor reads the color information in each pixel of the selected layer and the layer or background below it, and multiplies one color by the other color. The resulting color is always a darker color unless the top color is white—then it appears transparent. Since most of the blend modes are based on the mathematics used to calculate how the pixels are blended, they have really weird names like Linear Burn and Multiply. Many blend modes have unpredictable results, and the best way to use them is to experiment with them by previewing them.

Basic Color Correction—Be Very Careful

When working with color photos, it is important to determine what you want from the finished print. Do you want the color to be accurate, or do you want the colors to look good? It may surprise you to know that colors that are accurate don't always look as good. When I was visiting the Musée d'Orsay, I bought a lovely coffee-table book of the exhibit I was there to attend. While standing in front of a favorite painting by Claude Monet, I opened the book and compared it with the original. The lithograph in the book looked better than the original. Why? There are several possible reasons: the publishers may have wanted to show what the painting looked like when it was new; more likely they just wanted it to look good so more readers would buy the book. So, what is more important to you, color accuracy or the overall appeal of the finished work?

Color Casts and Their Causes

Most color problems people have with their photographs involve a *color cast* (also called a *shift*), which is a subtle but dominant color that is introduced into the photo. The favorite color cast of a sunny cloudless day is blue. This is because the subject is illuminated by a blue reflection of the clear sky, and while our eyes automatically adjust for this and we therefore don't notice it, the camera doesn't adjust. If the original was taken with a digital camera, color casts would have occurred when the automatic white balance (AWB) was tricked by large amounts of bright daylight.

Some light sources induce a desirable color cast. When your subject is illuminated by incandescent light, the resulting colors will shift toward the warm colors (always more appealing). A portrait that has a definite reddish-orange color cast appears more appealing, but taking away this particular color cast to make the photo's colors accurate would produce a much less desirable photo.

Color casts are difficult to remove. Even the automatic color correction of Photoshop Elements has little effect on the blue cast that dominates daytime photographs.

Correct Color Casts

Now that you understand color casts a little better, let's see how we can get rid of them. The first place to begin is the automatic color correction tools.

Use Photoshop Elements

If you are using Photoshop Elements, you can apply Auto Levels and Auto Contrast. You might be surprised that I didn't suggest you first try Auto Color Correction. In most cases, using Auto Color Correction doesn't change anything; in fact, it has been my experience that many times it makes the color cast of the photo worse.

Usually, application of Auto Levels and/or Auto Contrast will be all you need to do. Does this mean Auto Color Correction doesn't work? Not at all. It does mean that after you apply any automatic correction, you should look at the result, and decide if it helped or hindered the color-correction process. While Auto Color Correction may not work on one photo, it may work well on others.

Use Paint Shop Pro

Paint Shop Pro (PSP) offers several automatic color-correction tools that work quite well. But when I want to remove color casts, my tool of choice is the Manual Color Correction feature. In the dialog box for Manual Color Correction, I wanted to remove a bluish cast on the skin color of Jonathan and Grace that was caused by taking the photo in the late afternoon with a flash (very cool light). With PSP I only needed to select a small portion of Grace's forehead, as shown next, and then to pick a warmer skin tone color from a group of presets—pretty slick and only their skin color was adjusted, since the rest of the photo was unaffected by the flash.

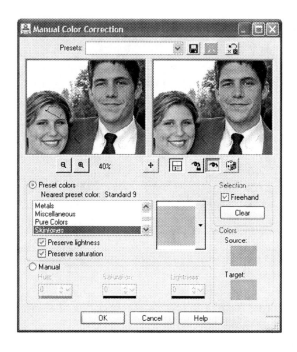

Help Automatic Tools Do a Better Job

When any automatic tool is applied to an image, the contents of the entire image are evaluated by the image editor, and then the correction is applied based on the information that was extracted from the photograph. In some cases, all of this information may cause a poor automatic adjustment to be made. In other situations, the proper application of color correction to one range of colors may cause another range of colors to look worse. In both cases, it sometimes is necessary to isolate one part of a photograph from the other using a selection. To recount what we learned about selections in the previous chapter, when we want to edit a particular area of your image without affecting other areas, you select the area you want to change.

Remove Red Eye from Photos

Red eye is a major problem for anyone taking photos with a flash. We all have had one photo or another that was ruined by red eye rearing its ugly eyes. It is caused by the flash reflecting off the retina of the person you are photographing (Figure 14-12). I think it is made more frustrating by cameras that have an anti–red-eye feature (which rarely works as advertised). For the record, a few things that help reduce red

FIGURE 14-12   Red eye has been a problem for photographers ever since the flash was invented.

eye are using an external flash or taking the photo in a well-lit room. Also, it helps if the subject is sober—no kidding.

It has been my experience that some people are really prone to red eye, and no matter what you do, you get the demon eye. So, to get rid of the red eye, we need to turn to the red-eye removal tool that is found in most image editors.

Paint Shop Pro's Red-Eye Removal Tool

Of all the built-in tools for removing red eye that are available in image editors, my favorite is the one found in Paint Shop Pro. When you select the Red-Eye Removal tool, a large dialog box (shown next) opens. Although it appears complicated, it isn't.

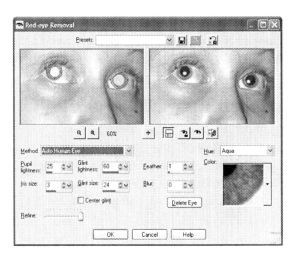

To remove red eye, select Auto Human Eye (they also have an Auto Animal Eye setting), pick the general eye color (aqua, gray, brown, and so on) that matches the subject, and then from a visual gallery, you can select almost an exact match. Drag the tool over the red eye in the left original window, and the result appears in the right preview window. It doesn't get any better than that.

> **TIP** *This is not the time to change the subject's eye color. You should always do your best to match the eye color correctly, or viewers who know the subject will look at the photo and think (they never say) that something's not quite right about the photo, though they may not be able to tell you what is wrong.*

Photoshop Elements' Red-Eye Brush Tool

Unlike Paint Shop Pro's automatic tool, The Red-Eye Brush tool in Photoshop Elements uses a much more manual approach. You select the color that is to be removed by clicking the actual red eye in the image. Next you pick the custom replacement color; this is the color that the eye is supposed to be. Click the Replacement color swatch in the Options bar, and pick the color that you want to use for the correction. Click the parts of the red eye that you want to correct, and paint over the red eye. Any pixels that match the target color are colorized with the replacement eye color.

The Red-Eye Removal Plug-in Filter

The one image editor that doesn't have a red-eye removal tool is Photoshop—go figure. Andromeda (www.andromeda.com) offers a RedEyePro plug-in filter (shown next) that automates the red-eye removal process.

14

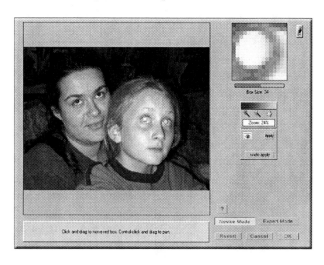

Sharpening Your Work

After you are happy with the color and other adjustments you have made to the photo, you can sharpen it. Here are a few things to know about sharpening photos. First, if the photo is out of focus, after you apply sharpening, it will still be out of focus. Second, while all image editors offer several different types of sharpening, you should ignore all of them except for Unsharp Mask. See the Did You Know box "What Is an Unsharp Mask?" Last point before we proceed: if you change the size of the photo, don't apply sharpening until you have the image at its final size.

When to Sharpen—During the Scan or Later?

You may hear the argument that you should always apply sharpening when performing the scan. This is true when you are using a high-end drum scanner (the kind that costs more than your house), but for a majority of scanners, use their default sharpen settings. If your scanner produces particularly noisy scans (as indicated by tiny rainbow-colored specks on the scanned image), you may want to turn the sharpening off altogether and see if that helps. So much for general information about sharpening; let's see how it is done.

The last correction you should apply to your photograph is sharpening.

What Is an Unsharp Mask?

Most people agree that the name "Unsharp Mask" (USM) filter sounds weird. The name is taken from the mechanical process that dates back at least 50 years. Nearly every image editor has this filter. Although the name may vary, it will have the word "unsharp" in it. Silly name or not, the USM filter is capable of applying sharpening to an image without producing the blowouts normally associated with excessive sharpening. The Unsharp Mask filter works by evaluating the contrast between adjacent pixels, and increasing that contrast when it's relatively high. The idea is that a large contrast difference between adjacent pixels usually represents an edge. But the filter doesn't really recognize edges, just pixel differences, so successful sharpening requires finding the settings that accentuate the edges in the image in a natural-looking way.

How Sharp Is Sharp Enough?

So, how much sharpening should you apply? It depends on what you are sharpening. Don't you just love that answer? I should run for a political office. It is true, though. If you are sharpening a portrait of an older person, sharpening will bring out all of the detail (wrinkles) in the face, so you might not want too much, if any, sharpening. If you are applying sharpening to artificial objects like buildings or cars, you can get away with almost any amount. You know you have applied too much sharpening when lighter parts of the image begin to lose their detail and become solid white. To demonstrate, Figure 14-13 is the original photo taken at a public performance in Mexico. Figure 14-14 has a moderate amount of sharpening applied using the Unsharp Mask filter. Figure 14-15 has an insane amount of sharpening applied, and you will notice that the areas of higher contrast have gone pure white. This phenomenon is called a *blowout* and should be avoided.

Another potential problem when sharpening a photograph that was scanned is that sharpening emphasizes all of the dust, hair, and other debris on the photo or scanner glass. This is especially noticeable if it is a photo that has a lot of dark areas—like someone wearing dark clothes, or a flash photo that produces a dark background. Apply too much sharpening to a photo like that, and it will appear that the photograph has developed a case of dandruff. Sometimes, even a moderate amount of sharpening can light up all of the debris that you should have cleaned

14

FIGURE 14-13   Original photo without sharpening

FIGURE 14-14   A mild amount of sharpening has been applied using the USM filter.

off the photograph and/or scanner before scanning. Figure 14-16 is a slightly out of focus photograph of our daughter, Grace. This photo was handled by many family members over the years and it is really dirty. When even moderate sharpening is applied (Figure 14-17), it results in the dirt and debris becoming much more

FIGURE 14-15   Applying too much sharpening creates an ugly photo.

FIGURE 14-16   This is a dirty picture, but the dirt and debris isn't too obvious.

apparent. You should also be aware that problems caused by oversharpening are more apparent in black-and-white (grayscale) photographs than in color ones.

Be careful of being seduced into adding too much contrast or sharpening. A quick glance at a photo that has either been given too much contrast or excessive

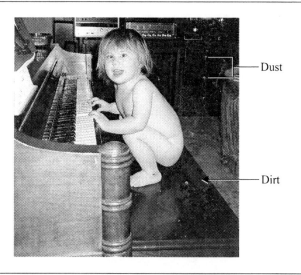

— Dust

— Dirt

14

FIGURE 14-17   Applying a moderate amount of sharpening really brings out the dirt.

sharpening gives the impression that it is more vivid. In fact, if you look back at the original, you will discover that a lot of detail in the photo has been lost. An exception to this is when you are applying contrast or sharpening artificial objects, like fancy metal work, buildings, and so on. When large amounts of sharpening are applied to these kinds of objects, it brings out the details and the textures. You must still be careful not to apply too much—even to artificial objects.

Covering a Lot of Material

We have covered a lot of topics in this chapter. It has taken me years to stuff all of that information into my brain, so I would not expect you to be able to absorb it in a single reading. What I suggest in my classes is to take one topic (like correcting color casts) and using your favorite image editor, experiment with different settings on several photos. Do your experimentation when you have some spare time, not when you are under a deadline.

In the next chapter, we will learn about using your image editor to repair photos. Physical damage to old photos is quite common; some pictures have been sitting in a drawer or a box for years, where they have been picked up and handled hundreds of times. Over the years these photos will get stained with ink, they will crack, and in some cases will even rip. You will discover that repairing them isn't as hard as you might think.

Chapter 15

Repair and Restore Photographs

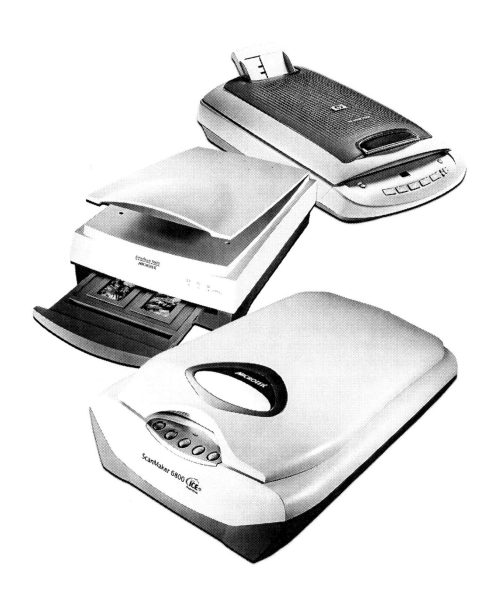

How to...

- Scan in photos for restoration and preservation
- Repair tears and creases in photos
- Restore faded photos
- Clean up dirty photos

There is no time like the present when it comes to scanning photographs and any other media. The older they get, the less information can be recovered from the image. Once the photograph has been saved and stored in the computer, you have stopped the aging of the scanned copy, and as you will learn in this chapter, you can reverse the damage done by time and mishandling.

Prepare to Restore Photos

When you are scanning an image for the purpose of restoring it, you will need to make a few adjustments to your normal scanning routine. First, if the photo or image that you are scanning is really old (as most of the examples in this chapter are), it is fragile. Therefore, you should exercise caution when handling and preparing it for scanning.

General Print Handling Procedures and Precautions

Always hold prints or negatives by their edges. Do not touch the surface unless you are wearing cotton gloves; even clean fingers can leave natural skin oil secretions that can damage a photo over time. You can get cotton gloves specially made for handling photos at your local camera store.

Don't mark the back of your photo permanently in any way. The chemicals in some markers (especially a laundry marker) will eventually find their way to the other side of the photograph and ruin it. If you must make a temporary identification, write brief information gently with only a very soft 2B or 4B pencil.

Never repair a photograph by applying adhesive tape to it. I saw the Dead Sea scrolls last year, and one of the archivists told me a major restoration task for the past five years was removing the adhesive tape that the original curators used to piece together the scrolls. If you have a photo that is in several pieces, keep all of the pieces in a clean, chemically inert (also called *pH neutral*) polyester bag or sleeve.

Scan for Restoration

This section contains guidelines for scanning photographs and other documents specifically for restoration and preservation. They differ from normal scanning guidelines in several ways.

Enlarge the Original

As a general rule, make images destined for restoration result in a final scan twice the original size. For example, a 4×6" print should be scanned at a setting of 200 percent to create a final scanned image of 8×12". The quickest way to do this is by using a typical Resize command from within your scanning software, such as the one shown next.

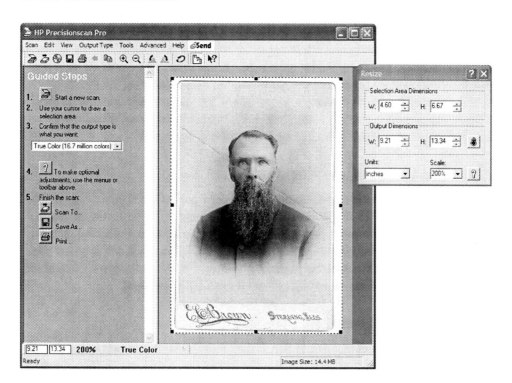

15

By doubling the size of the original, you are forcing the scanner to capture the maximum amount of detail in the original photo and giving yourself more area and pixels to work with. An exception to this rule is if the original is really small, you should consider using an even larger resize factor (like 300–500 percent). If the original image is so huge that it covers the entire scanner glass, then 100 percent will probably be sufficient. Chapter 14 tells how to resize the photo using the scanning software.

Use the Highest-Quality Scan Setting

You want to capture the maximum possible amount of image detail from the scanned image without worrying about how big the final file will be. For photos and memorabilia that you want to preserve, scan in the original as RGB (24-bit) color. Black-and-white photos in most cases should be scanned in as grayscale, the exception being if they have been hand-colored or have a colored stain on them. Preserving the color in such cases allows isolation of the stain using color-sensitive selection tools.

If the original has some tonal problems (too dark, faded) you may want to make some minor image adjustments as explained in Chapter 10. If you have scanned in the entire photo, frame and all, the color of the frame may have influenced the autoexposure adjustment tools during the scan. To solve this, you should either select just the photo and try the automatic setting again, or manually adjust the tonal settings. Just remember to evaluate tonal or color adjustments made with the scanner with an image editor or a file viewer and not from the preview window in the scanner software—which is a poor representation of the image.

Scan the Original—Warts and All

When scanning for preservation, do not crop out any part of the original. Figure 15-1 is a photo taken in 1928 that was glued to a stained paper frame. I have scanned the entire photo and, in most cases, will even include a little extra around the edges. When you get around to actually restoring the photo, you can crop out the frame from a copy of the scanned photo, but you always want to preserve the entire original so you have a visual record of how it originally appeared.

Store Using a Lossless File Format

Do not save the original as a JPEG file. For restoration work, you should not save the images you are working on using any file format that uses *lossy* file compression. This includes Wavelet, JPEG, and JPEG 2000. Lossy file compression degrades the image. Probably the most popular graphic format to use is TIFF, and you can choose one of several compression options that are *lossless,* meaning they do not degrade the image. Be careful not to choose the JPEG compression option that is now available as a choice for JPEG.

FIGURE 15-1   Though the paper frame is in poor shape, it is important to scan it all.

Repair Tears and Creases

One of the more common problems with old photos is that they have not usually received museum-quality care and storage. Unprotected, the important images can easily become bent, folded, and otherwise damaged. Physically, there isn't anything that can be done for the original (with the exception of work done by a restoration specialist), but it's relatively easy to repair an electronic version and then to print it.

The damage caused by folding a photograph depends on its age and the material it is printed on. Photos taken in the past decade are printed on a flexible Mylar that can stand almost any degree of contortion, while photos printed around the turn of the 20th century were printed on stiff material, and in most cases even a slight bend produces a hard, raised crease from which the image may flake off, as in the example shown in Figure 15-2.

15

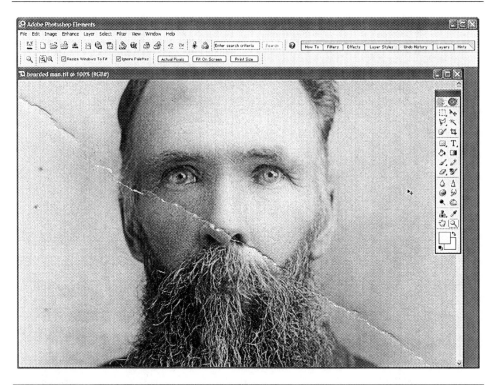

FIGURE 15-2 At 100% the image doesn't fit in the image window, but it accurately shows the damage that must be repaired.

Here is the step-by-step procedure to repair a crease from an old photograph:

1. After ensuring the scanner glass is clean, position the original photo on the center of the scanner glass. Run a preview scan and change the output size so the resulting scan is twice as large (200%) as the original.

2. Save the scan using a unique name, and save a second separate copy under a different name (for example, with the suffix "copy") using the Save As command.

3. When you open the copy, make sure that the image editor view is set to 100%, as shown in Figure 15-2. In Photoshop and Photoshop Elements,

this is called "Actual Pixels." Because of the large size of the image, only a portion of it will be visible in the image window. When doing retouching and restoration work, it is often necessary to get in real close (200–400%) to fix the image, but you must always return to 100% to accurately evaluate the changes made.

4. Select the Clone Brush tool, and change the brush settings to a soft-edged brush. We'll start with the most distracting part of the defect, the crease that is running across the man's face. Select a spot near the crease as the sample point for the clone brush, and then just dab spots along the crease using single mouse clicks (rather than holding down the mouse button and dragging the brush) along the crease. Dragging the clone brush makes a visible line that isn't as bad as the original crease, but it still looks like someone has been tinkering with the photo. Change the sample point often (using either side of the crease) to avoid repeating patterns. In the following image, I have cloned out part of the crease running across the face, leaving part of it so you could tell where it used to be.

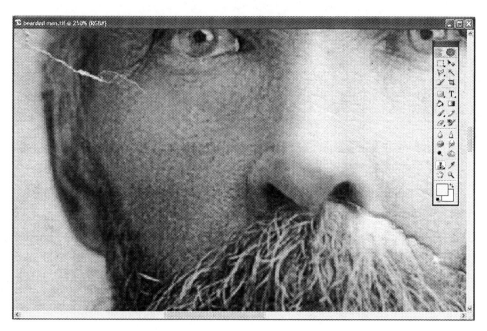

15

5. When working on critical areas (like the crease across the face), zoom in as much as necessary to be able to use the smallest soft-edged clone brush to get the small areas. You can see in the image shown next that I am working at a magnification of 340%, so I use a smaller brush to get in and around the tear that went through the nostril.

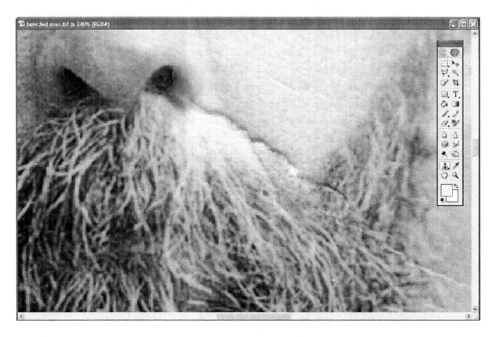

6. Use the clone brush to remove the remaining parts of the crease and some of the dark spots on the background.

7. Return to either 100% or Fit to Window zoom level to see how the entire image looks.

8. This particular image had developed a sepia tint from its age, so I opened the Levels dialog box (shown next) in Photoshop Elements (CTRL-L).

Selecting the White Point eyedropper (on the right), I clicked the part of the original border of the photograph that would have been the whitest part when it was new. The finished image is shown in Figure 15-3.

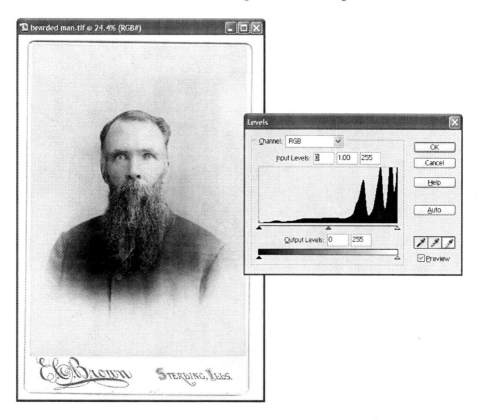

9. To complete the work, resize the image to return it to its correct size. A natural softening of the image results from making it smaller. This can sometimes make a harsh image look better. If it softens it too much, apply the Unsharp Mask filter at a low setting.

15

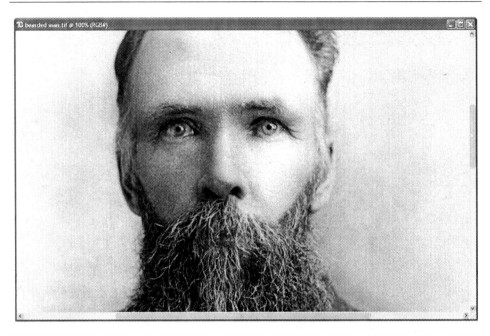

FIGURE 15-3   Using the clone tool, it is a simple matter to remove even the worst damage.

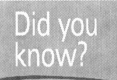

What's a Clone Tool?

Most image editors have a clone tool, although not all of them specifically use the name "clone." Until version 5, the clone tool in Photoshop was called the "rubber stamp" tool. Now it's called the Clone Stamp tool. Most other image editors call it a "clone tool" or "clone brush." Regardless of what you call it, they all do the same thing. The clone tool takes a sample from designated points of an image, which can then be painted onto another image or different parts of the same image. The user selects a sample point on the image and then moves the clone brush to the desired area of the image and begins applying copies of pixels from the sample point to the area under the clone brush.

Restore a Paper Frame

While the clone tool or brush is a great tool, other solutions are available for repairing and restoring a scanned image. The paper frame or paper matte (shown next) in which the photo was mounted has seen much use and abuse.

In this restoration we are going to specify portions of one part of the frame to make sections to cover another. Here is how it is done using Photoshop Elements, but the same technique can be performed with almost any image editor:

1. With the image loaded in your image editor, change the view to 100% (Actual Pixels). As seen next, the lower-left corner has two serious stains, so that's where we'll start.

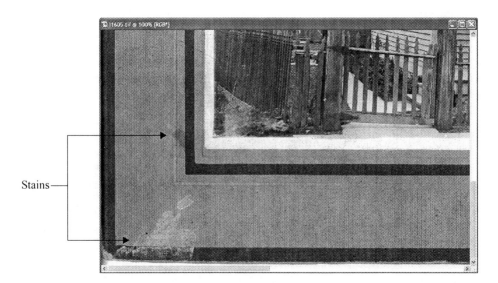

Stains

2. Select an area of the frame that is clean, create a rectangle selection, and put a feathered edge on the selection like the one shown next. The feathering of the selection produces gradual transitions so our patchwork isn't visible. Because this is a large image, the 5-pixel feather I have chosen will produce a very small transition area.

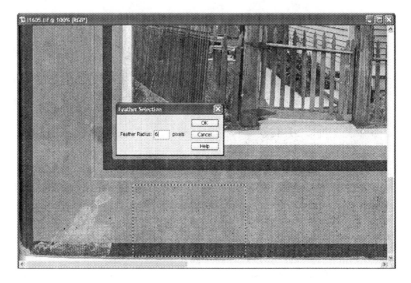

3. In Elements, select the Move tool (V), and while holding down the ALT key and the SHIFT key, drag the selection to the left until it covers the bad spot on the corner, as shown in Figure 15-4. The ALT key makes a copy of the selection (rather than replacing it with the background color). The SHIFT

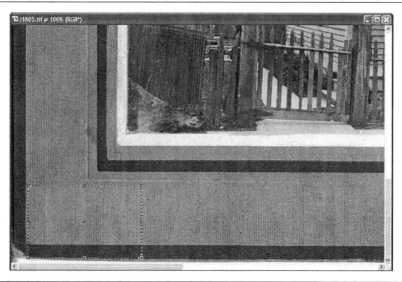

FIGURE 15-4   Moving a selection over the stain easily and quickly covers the paint stain.

key is a constraint key that prevents the selection from moving up or down, making alignment much easier.

4. Remove the selection (CTRL-D) and continue making more selections to repair all of the stains on the paper frame. To remove the other stain, I set the selection tool to automatically make a selection with a 6-pixel feather, as shown next.

15

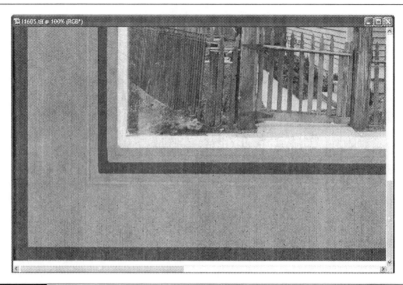

FIGURE 15-5   Using floating selections allowed stains to be quickly removed.

5.   The final step was to make a hard-edged selection (no feather) of the dark
     edge border to rebuild the worn corner of the print. The finished corner is
     shown in Figure 15-5.

Clean Up Dirty Backgrounds

Just like the frame we repaired in the previous section, a dirty background can be
repaired with a clone tool or brush, but it would take too much time. So, we are
going to learn how to clean up the debris in the background of a photo taken way
back in 1897 (Figure 15-6).

This procedure is shown using Paint Shop Pro 8, but it will work on most
major image editors since the tools (or their equivalent) are found in most major
photo editors. Here is how to clean up a dirty sky in the sample photo:

1.   Open the image and using a freehand selection tool, select part or all of
     the background that you want to clean. In the image shown next, I used
     the Edge Seeker tool, which allowed me to rapidly create the selection
     composed of the background of the image.

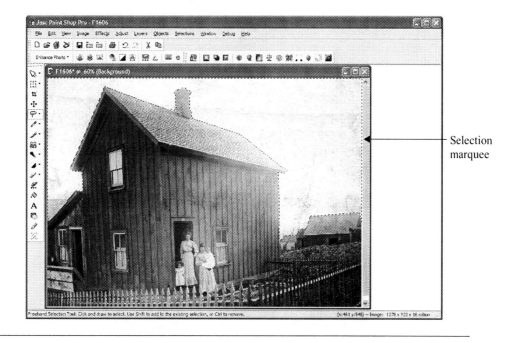

Selection marquee

FIGURE 15-6   This photo is over 100 years old and looks like it has a hundred years of dirt and scratches on it.

2. With the background selected, you can remove the dust and debris in several ways. You can just press DEL, and the background will become pure white (assuming your background color is set to white). This will produce an artificial-looking backdrop and draw the viewer's attention. If you are using Photoshop, you can use the dust and scratch filters at a high setting to remove the debris while leaving a background that appears to be part of the original print. In Paint Shop Pro 8, I used Gamma Adjustment to lighten it up sufficiently to effectively remove the dirty look of the sky so it appears to be part of the original photo, as shown next.

To be honest, there was as much debris on the house walls as there was in the sky. Since the dust and scratches are dark, they don't really stand out, so I left them. To finish working on the photo, I did a few things that have nothing to do with cleaning up the background. First, I inverted the selection that was made and used Paint Shop Pro's Darken brush to make the chimney and right side of the roof darker. To do the same in Photoshop or Photoshop Elements, use the Burn tool set to midtones and a light opacity (10–15%). Figure 15-7 shows the final image, which is—as we say in Texas—all dressed up and ready for church.

FIGURE 15-7   Another photograph that has been rescued before it suffered any more damage

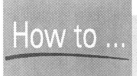 **Unroll a Panorama Photo**

A popular way to take class and other group photographs is to make a panorama. These photos that have been rolled or folded for long periods resist opening, and some could even be damaged if forced open. Introducing moisture through humidification, followed by careful flattening, allows documents to safely return to a flat state. Humidification also reduces creases and fold lines that distort the image during scanning.

There are several ways to relax the document with humidity. I have a neighbor with a hothouse, and he lets me leave rolled photos I am working on in a box with holes in it for a couple of days free of charge. If you don't

15

have a hothouse friend and the photo isn't too brittle, you can easily make a device that will both humidify and flatten documents.

To flatten a rolled document, you will need to make what is called a *sandwich* (low calorie). Several archivists I met during the course of writing this book used this technique. The idea is to create a multilayer stack, see the following illustration, with moist layers that do not physically come into contact with the photo or document you want to relax but that allow the humidity to affect it through osmosis. Here is how you make it:

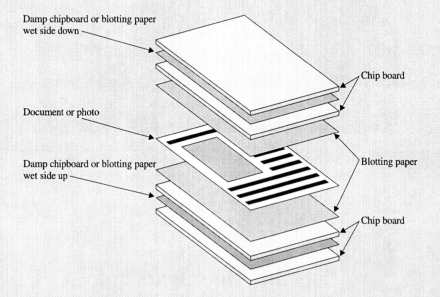

Damp chipboard or blotting paper wet side down

Chip board

Document or photo

Blotting paper

Damp chipboard or blotting paper wet side up

Chip board

1. Place a sheet of chipboard or blotting paper on a flat surface (glass, Plexiglas, or wood).

2. Take a second sheet of chipboard, place it under a faucet, and run water on it. You're not trying to soak it, just get it wet.

3. Shake off the excess water, and lay this sheet on top of the first piece, wet side up.

4. Place a third, dry sheet of chipboard on the stack, followed by a sheet of blotting paper or silicon quick-release paper.

5. On top of this stack unroll the document(s) to be humidified. You may need some help holding the document down since the reason you are doing this is that the photo doesn't want to stay unrolled.

6. Now place either a second sheet of blotter paper or silicone release paper on top of the document.

7. Make a second blotting paper/chipboard stack—like the first one, but with the wet side down—for the top, so that the photo is in the middle.

8. Place another sheet of glass, wood, or Plexiglas on top, and then place weights on it.

9. If the documents are not dry and flat after 48 hours, repeat the process. Make sure the flattened photo is dry before putting it away—flat this time.

All of the supplies needed to make this sandwich are available at your local arts and crafts or hobby store.

Another Way to Remove Stains

With all of this advice on stain and dirt removal, I am wondering if I can get a guest spot on Martha Stewart's show. The stain in the image shown next is usually caused by a clear oil such as mineral oil or sewing machine oil. What makes this type of stain unique is that it darkens the color, but the stain is basically transparent. The placement of the stain on the oval paper frame pattern prevents placing a selection over it as we did earlier in the chapter. In this case, we will isolate the stain with a selection and tweak the hue, saturation, and lightness. Here is how it is done:

1. Use the Magic Wand tool, set to a low tolerance, and select the stain. You will need to play with the tolerance until you get the correct setting. Check the settings for your Magic Wand tool if your selection includes areas isolated from the stain. Most Magic Wand tools have one setting that allows them to select all pixels that are contiguous to the starting point or another setting that selects all similar colors in the image. You want it set so it only selects pixels that are contiguous to the starting point. With a little tweaking, you should end up with a selection like the one shown next that accurately outlines the stain.

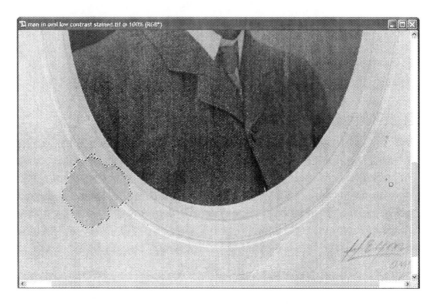

NOTE *Don't put a feather on your stain selection. If you do, it will result in a faint outline of the stain when you are done.*

2. Once you have the selection the way you want it, hide the marquee (CTRL-ALT-H works on both Elements and Paint Shop Pro) and open the Hue/Saturation dialog box (CTRL-U) shown next.

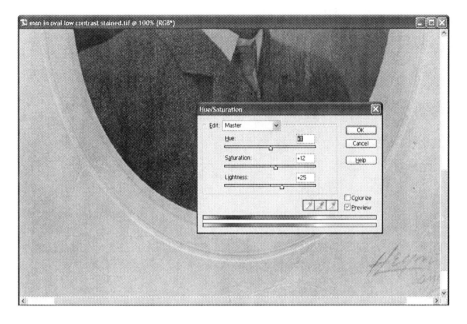

3. Adjust the Lightness until it appears to be as light as the surrounding area. You will notice that the color inside the section will not appear to be as vivid as the area outside. No problem—move the Saturation controls up slightly until the stain disappears. A very slight fringe will always mark part of the original stain edge. We'll fix that in the next step.

4. For final cleanup, remove the selection (CTRL-D). Use a clone brush to remove any edges of the stain that remain. I also got rid of the small stain above the big stain with the same method. Last thing to do is to get rid of smaller defects or other junk like the dirty smudge that was barely visible above the stain. The best stain remover tool for that is the Dodge tool with a setting of Shadows at an exposure of approximately 10%. Paint Shop Pro users should use the Lighten tool at a low opacity. The cleaned-up paper frame is shown in Figure 15-8. Now all I need to do is call Martha.

15

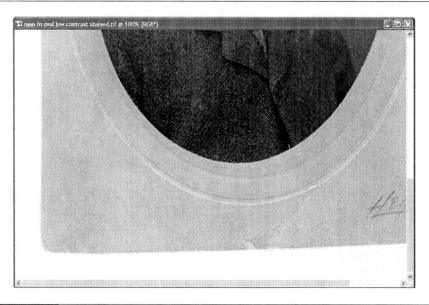

FIGURE 15-8   You and your image editor can easily remove a stubborn stain from any object.

We have covered some of the basics of image restoration in this chapter, and if time and page count allowed, we could go on for another 30 pages. It is so much fun to restore old photos and see how things used to look. At this point, I would tell you what was in the next chapter, but since this is the last chapter, I guess I will just thank you for buying the book and really hope that you learned something. Anytime I write a book, I always learn something new, and this book was no exception.

Cheers,
Dave Huss

Index

G

INTERNATIONAL CONTACT INFORMATION

AUSTRALIA
McGraw-Hill Book Company Australia Pty. Ltd.
TEL +61-2-9900-1800
FAX +61-2-9878-8881
http://www.mcgraw-hill.com.au
books-it_sydney@mcgraw-hill.com

CANADA
McGraw-Hill Ryerson Ltd.
TEL +905-430-5000
FAX +905-430-5020
http://www.mcgraw-hill.ca

GREECE, MIDDLE EAST, & AFRICA
(Excluding South Africa)
McGraw-Hill Hellas
TEL +30-210-6560-990
TEL +30-210-6560-993
TEL +30-210-6560-994
FAX +30-210-6545-525

MEXICO (Also serving Latin America)
McGraw-Hill Interamericana Editores S.A. de C.V.
TEL +525-117-1583
FAX +525-117-1589
http://www.mcgraw-hill.com.mx
fernando_castellanos@mcgraw-hill.com

SINGAPORE (Serving Asia)
McGraw-Hill Book Company
TEL +65-863-1580
FAX +65-862-3354
http://www.mcgraw-hill.com.sg
mghasia@mcgraw-hill.com

SOUTH AFRICA
McGraw-Hill South Africa
TEL +27-11-622-7512
FAX +27-11-622-9045
robyn_swanepoel@mcgraw-hill.com

SPAIN
McGraw-Hill/Interamericana de España, S.A.U.
TEL +34-91-180-3000
FAX +34-91-372-8513
http://www.mcgraw-hill.es
professional@mcgraw-hill.es

UNITED KINGDOM, NORTHERN,
EASTERN, & CENTRAL EUROPE
McGraw-Hill Education Europe
TEL +44-1-628-502500
FAX +44-1-628-770224
http://www.mcgraw-hill.co.uk
computing_europe@mcgraw-hill.com

ALL OTHER INQUIRIES Contact:
Osborne/McGraw-Hill
TEL +1-510-549-6600
FAX +1-510-883-7600
http://www.osborne.com
omg_international@mcgraw-hill.com

New Offerings from Osborne's
How to Do Everything Series

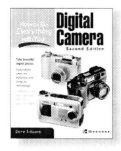

How to Do Everything with Your Digital Camera, 2nd Edition
ISBN: 0-07-222555-6

How to Do Everything with Photoshop Elements 2
ISBN: 0-07-222638-2

How to Do Everything with Photoshop 7
ISBN: 0-07-219554-1

How to Do Everything with Your Sony CLIÉ
ISBN: 0-07-222659-5

How to Do Everything with Your Scanner
ISBN: 0-07-219106-6

How to Do Everything with Your Palm™ Handheld, 3rd Edition
ISBN: 0-07-222528-9

How to Do Everything with Your Tablet PC
ISBN: 0-07-222771-0

How to Do Everything with Your iPod
ISBN: 0-07-222700-1

How to Do Everything with Your iMac, 3rd Edition
ISBN: 0-07-213172-1

How to Do Everything with Your iPAQ Pocket PC
ISBN: 0-07-222333-2

  OSBORNE
www.osborne.com

Printed in the United States
68837LVS00004B/66

9 780072 228915